BEYOND THE PAIN

Transforming Grief and Disappointment into Growth and Healing

MADHUR-NAIN WEBSTER, LMFT

Hatherleigh Press, Ltd.

62545 State Highway 10

Hobart, NY 13788, USA

hatherleighpress.com

Beyond the Pain

Library of Congress Cataloging-in-Publication Data is available.

ISBN: 978-1-961293-29-8

Printed in the United States

The authorized representative in the EU for product safety and compliance is Catarina Astrom, Blästorpsvägen 14, 276 35 Borrby, Sweden. info@hatherleighpress.com

10 9 8 7 6 5 4 3 2 1

Disclaimer: The information in this book is for educational purposes only. This information is not to be treated as therapy nor medical advice. This book is a generalized program for the mass population.

PRAISE FOR *BEYOND THE PAIN*

"*Beyond the Pain* offers a compassionate and insightful exploration of the complex journey through grief. The book forges a path forward, a movement beyond the immediate suffering towards a place of growth and healing. I strongly recommend to anyone who is wounded and seeking peace beyond the pain."

— Delta Ruscheinsky, MD

"*Beyond the Pain* is a perfect self-gift for anyone who finds themselves ruminating over a disappointment or loss, big or small. With a clear and practical voice, combined with humor and self-disclosure, Madhur-Nain walks through the process of moving through grief and disappointment. Disappointment is a universal experience, but it comes in many shades, and I expect every reader will find much to resonate with in any number of the stages."

—Cathy Hill, PhD, registered psychologist

"*Beyond the Pain* embraces the complexities of emotional injury and loss with humanity and humility. It empowers readers to compassionately and powerfully embrace their pain and fosters emotional resilience and wholeness. It is a deeply insightful read, and one that provides practical support in healing."

—Alison Buckley, LMFT, Professor of Psychology, Yuba College

"Written with equal parts empathy and insight, *Beyond the Pain* invites readers to redefine their narratives and encourages us to view setbacks as stepping stones toward resilience and a deeper self-acceptance. A must-read for anyone looking to rewrite their story during life's most challenging moments."

—Terry Real, *New York Times* bestselling author of *US*

This book is dedicated to my clients who have been paralyzed by drama and/or trauma in their lives. I have watched you put in the hard work and witnessed your healing process. Through your courage, I was inspired to write this book. I honor you. And I honor my inner child, who learned of the power of change after navigating through her own childhood trauma.

CONTENTS

PREFACE

THROUGHOUT MY 26-YEAR CAREER as a licensed marriage and family therapist, I have encountered countless couples seeking help on their life journey together. I have witnessed every imaginable perspective on relationships by observing my clients and the different outcomes of their choices. Although there have been many success stories, I have also helped guide couples through the heartbreak of dissolving a relationship.

Naturally, this is often enormously disappointing for my clients. To make matters more complicated, the experience can sometimes trigger grief from their pasts: the pain of dealing with parents, the uncertainties of youth, the fear of emotional growth (or lack thereof).

Disappointment, as we all know, comes in a myriad of forms beyond relationship grievances. It can happen when you don't land that dream job after you thought you nailed the interview, during a stressful vacation that isn't living up to your expectations, or from a partner who is withdrawing from you emotionally or physically. It could even be because your favorite sports team lost the championship game. (Sorry, Toronto Maple Leafs—your day will come!) Disappointments can be big or small, life-altering or mildly inconvenient, within your control or out of it. It can take the form of horrific news about a loved one, or something as silly and innocuous (in hindsight) as an overcooked burger.

The point is, we all know how it feels when something doesn't go our way. These setbacks are a part of life, whether we like it or not. Try as we might, we cannot avoid all irritants and displeasures.

So, if it's an ever-present and natural part of life, what's the big deal?

We all experience disappointment in our lives, but we don't all experience it in the same way. When disappointment transforms itself into lingering grief, it can fester and threaten to disturb—or even destroy—your life. To avoid this, you must learn how to recognize the nefarious signs of harmful disappointment so that you can intercede for yourself *before* it causes lasting damage.

For all that, it is not always easy to address the intricacies of disappointment, particularly when it comes to something deeply personal. The separation from a partner or our parents not offering the love and reliability we need, for example, are sensitive subjects. Healing from this kind of pain takes time and dedication, as well as uniquely personal devotion to one's better health. I have written this book in hopes of giving you the support you will need as you parse through disappointment, in whatever form it may come, while trying to make sense of your grief.

My reason for doing so is simple: I love helping people and strive to do so to the best of my abilities. Being able to guide others on a path of self-healing—through acts of self-reflection to confront and deal with their issues—has long been a great privilege of mine. As Dr. Gabor Maté says, "If, in your early experience, someone taught you that you're not enough, then one of the ways of compensating for that is to become a helper."* I have worked through my own grief. I have learned how to be unattached to the outcome while maintaining a big heart and gentle power. My combined knowledge and experience have given me wisdom that I am keen to share with others. In fact, the seed of this book came

---

* *Psychotherapy Networker* (2021)

from a desire to extend my knowledge beyond my clients and to help as many people as possible. I hope I can help you, too.

Like you, I have experienced my own share of disappointments. But, upon reflection, I've recognized that I learned from each of those experiences and come out stronger in the end. I want to reassure you that it *is* possible to find a sense of growth and even joy in the aftermath of disappointment. You may change a little or a lot in the process, but you can eventually heal through this transformation. You can create action through grief. You have this ability within you...*if* you're willing to put in the work.

With courage and determination, I know your journey will continue, even if it may be a little different from what you expected.

Welcome to *Beyond the Pain*.

With love and respect,
Madhur-Nain

CHAPTER 1

RECOGNIZING DISAPPOINTMENT

THE MOMENT WE ARE born, we experience our first form of disappointment. The shock to our system as we move from the warm confines of a soft womb into the cold, bright white lights of a delivery room is a lot for our young bodies and nervous systems to handle. We feel unsure, drawing comfort only from familiar voices around us. This sense of unease is our first brush with disappointment, and so our journey of living begins.

To live is to be active: to accept the push and pull of what draws us in or keeps us away. Emerging from the womb is a push, while the bond we forge with our parents is a pull. Children are hardwired to form attachments with their caretakers; as adults, we're not much different. Human beings crave connection, whether with groups, other individuals, or even our pets. Yet in pursuing our innate want to be connected to other living beings, we will unavoidably experience pain; this can occur when a relationship ends or because someone has passed away. Life is about overcoming the hurdles of grief caused by disappointment—not by passively avoiding them, but by actively maneuvering through these obstacles. I often tell my clients, "It is not what happens to us but how we make sense of it."

Sometimes, disappointments charge in and change the course of our lives, like the loss of a loved one or experiencing traumatic abuse of some kind. Shocking events like these contribute to the formation of our "story" and shift our perspective on life. The ripple effects stirred up by these experiences can shape our feelings and alter our faith in others and in ourselves, including our own choices.

Depending on what we do with our new insight, these changes may not always be bad. Unfortunately, most of us have not been taught to view disappointing moments in our lives as opportunities to pause, learn, pivot, and grow. It makes sense; most of us are young when we first experience the sorts of big disappointments that can affect and influence our lives. The divorce of parents, for example, often happens when we are in the reactive phase of our development. Children, teens, and young adults do not commonly have the ability to take personal timeouts and assess potential next steps.

Responding rationally, rather than reacting irrationally, is a learned behavior that is strengthened with age and experience. Disappointments—and their aftershocks—shape our identities, emotionally, spiritually, and physically. We must learn to work with and understand each new narrative so that we can better write (and, if necessary, rewrite) our own story.

We must learn to *"be"* with what has happened in order to properly process the disappointments in our life. You must embrace the concept that what you are thinking is only your interpretation of what is happening around you; it may not always be real or true. You must embrace the fact that you have a choice in how you react and/or respond to any given situation. This is easier said than done, but it is worth putting in the work and learning how to adopt this behavior. **After all, we must be able to self-reflect so that we can self-correct.**

Disappointment as an Opportunity for Growth

Think of disappointments as moments where you are able to make big or small changes in your life. It can either be the end of something or the beginning of everything. It's like the age-old saying: "What doesn't kill you makes you stronger." Of course, that concept is not always easy to accept; it can be hard to see through your pain, especially when it is fresh or especially severe. It often seems unthinkable to ever reach the other side of grief, the side that is healed and full of promise.

In *The Coddling of the American Mind* (2018), authors Greg Lukianoff and Jonathan Haidt discuss how we are raising children to think, "What hurts me can kill me." This mentality has trained children and young adults to be overly sensitive and reactive. They do not know how to experience and process difficult feelings; they don't even have the ability to initiate difficult conversations. By avoiding pain, we deny ourselves the opportunity to sit with our emotions and learn how to handle them. **Only by recognizing all facets of our emotions—even the painful ones—can we embark on a path to change, acceptance, and ultimately, joy.**

Time plays a big part in the healing process or when moving past disappointment in general, no matter its magnitude. Only you can decide when you are ready (or even able) to let go. In fact, part of the process is understanding that "letting go" means freeing yourself of your hurt, your anger, your loneliness. To let go is to release your current story, the false narrative you have written in your mind. Think of it like a bird that has been in a cage. Now the door has opened; the bird has the choice to fly out or remain trapped inside. Wouldn't it want to fly free?

If you continue holding onto your old pain, you will continue to live your life from inside that pain's point of view. This can cause many years of suffering, which can manifest internally (low self-esteem) or express itself externally (strained relationships). Holding onto this suffering will negatively impact your personality, your view of life, and your view of others around you.

When I was taking care of my grandfather throughout the last five years of his life, he reached a point where he had to be moved into a care facility. There was an elderly woman in her late 80s who would walk around the house with her baby doll and yell "shut up" at everyone she saw. At first, it made me giggle—but then I considered how she likely had never reconciled with the pain of her inner child. If we don't process and eventually let go of the story which holds our pain, it will resurface later in our life.

I hope this sparks a fire underneath you to put in the effort to heal, rather than allow your pain to serve as an anchor around your neck that only weighs you down, justification for feeling sorry for yourself, I hope that you can learn how to release the story of who you *think* you are and how you perceive life impacting you in order to justify your anger. We all have the capacity to move onwards after disappointment, even if it is one small step at a time.

WORKSHOP

Think of a painful old story/event that resurfaces every so often in your memory. Consider the feelings you associate with this event.

- What is your role in this memory? Were others involved in this event?

- How did you process this experience? Is it an ongoing process?

- Why do you hold onto this memory?

- If it was a consequential and life-changing event, how did it impact your life?

Whether it was a big or small disappointment, your life perspective will continue to be affected by this event until you are able to fully process the experience. If you have a strong reaction to this memory, make a note to yourself to revisit it while going through the healing stages later in this book. It may even trigger unwanted emotions that require additional attention from a licensed mental health professional. There is courage in recognizing when you might need extra support, so please do not hesitate to reach out.

Differing Reactions to Disappointment

We cannot avoid every single form of disappointment that may appear throughout our lives. In one way or another, disappointment will manifest and affect us to varying degrees. Some forms are more evident and hurt deeply, while others are almost entirely unnoticed. Why is that?

Why do some disappointments bother us and others don't? Is it that we have become numb due to constant exposure? Perhaps we have chosen to endure these moments by accepting them as just "being a part of life."

In truth, how we react to disappointments is directly influenced by our childhood experiences. For example, if a child tells a white lie which then blows up into a big issue, the child will *not* naturally learn to tell the truth next time. They require patience and understanding as they learn and grow—but someone needs to offer them that opportunity. They need guidance. **We are not born with the skill to reflect, after all.**

If you are a parent who feels guilty upon reading this, don't beat yourself up. We all make mistakes as parents because we all make mistakes as humans. The important thing to remember is it is never too late to set a better example. Our children learn the most through observed behavior, but it's not like that potential for learning stops the moment they become adults. The changes you make in your life will continue to impact your children, no matter their age. We never stop learning. My parents are in their mid-70s and are still reflecting, processing, recalibrating, and growing. The constant change keeps them young in body, mind, and spirit. In fact, their continual growth inspires me as I continue to reflect on my own life.

As I worked on this book, I kept coming across hidden disappointments in my personal history. I looked back at my own childhood and saw glimpses of missed opportunities because of the strict religious system in which I was raised. I remembered a time when I chose my boyfriend over my own path, only to have him dump me months later. I thought of a friend who never took the initiative to invite me to dinner, only the other way around. I reflected on the #MeToo movement in the community I grew up in, which affected people I was close to, and the mix of emotions that were stirred up as a result: deep pain, anger, sadness, and shame. By enduring each of these disappointments, did I grow as an individual? Has the community around me changed? Have these experiences forced me to look deep within myself and recognize my truth? To all three questions, I would earnestly say, "Yes."

Some disappointments are a healthy exercise in perseverance. A romantic breakup may be essential in order for you to get reacquainted with yourself or create space to make the life changes that are best for you. The loss of a friendship can pave the way for new, more positively influential people in your life. Losing your favorite shirt or gadget can be the universe's way of telling you to let go of attachments. **Even the death of a loved one, or some kind of loss on a community level, are grievances that allow us chances to heal, fortifying ourselves in the process.** Being let down by religion or politics or society at large can each be a chance to wake up to reality and readjust our expectations. They are all moments in our life's journey when we can stop and check in on ourselves and our perspectives.

How a situation impacts you will depend on your interpretation of it, which is why it is wise to spend time with your emotions. You, and only you, give your own emotions meaning. Consider this a call to action to reflect on what is important to you. What do you believe in? Do you want to leave the church? End the friendship? Dissolve the marriage? Quit the job? When we don't have a firm grip on the realities of a situation, we tend to go into reactive mode and attack the other parties involved, yet nothing good can come without first being objective, sitting with ourselves, and self-reflecting.

I know revisiting disappointments may make you feel angry, sad, or depressed, but in each of these situations you give yourself the space to reevaluate your morals, your wants, your needs, your own character. Facing disappointment in life is like holding a mirror up to yourself. Observe how you look, how you respond. You can either take the time to sit with the disappointment and use it as an opportunity to transform and grow, or you can get lost in the pain of your personal story, drowning in thoughts of, "It's not fair." How do you respond to disappointment? How do you *want* to respond to disappointment? What do you want to see when you look in the mirror? How do you want your life to be?

WORKSHOP

Take some time to think of a few disappointing moments you have experienced, starting from as early in your life as you can remember and working your way to today. Write down at least five of these moments. They can be big ("My partner and I were/are incompatible") or small ("My online order didn't arrive when they said it would"). Write down your reflections, conclusions, and general feelings regarding these various scenarios. You can look at the following questions for guidance:

- How did your parental figure(s) react to disappointments, big and small? How did they react to loss or mistakes?

- Did anyone in your childhood talk about disappointments?

- Some of the primary emotions I work with when helping clients process their feelings include joy, love, shame, guilt, pain, anger, and fear. Which were the most expressed emotions in your family? Which emotions, if any, were avoided?

- How did you learn about anger as a child?

- When you were young, what did "safe" mean to you?

- What are you most afraid of? How or when did you learn to be afraid? Why do you think you are afraid of this?

- How did you find meaning in yourself in your youth? How do you find meaning in yourself as an adult?

Reconciling Bad Things Happening in Life

There is a commonly held belief throughout the world that if you are good, follow the rules, and do the right thing, then nothing bad will happen to you. Many religions preach this notion; some call it *karma* or chalk it up to, "What goes around, comes around." Some even take it the extra step further, thinking, "If I am good, only good things will happen to me and for me."

My friends, this is sadly not the case.

Everything and nothing can happen to anyone and everyone, good and bad. There are no guarantees in life—not for success, love, money, friendships, health, or a family. Sure, sometimes what goes around *will* come around, but this is not a reflection of someone's pious nature (or lack thereof). If you or a loved one gets cancer, it's not because you didn't pray enough. If your business partner secretly embezzles your company's savings, it's not because you didn't do enough good service towards others. If your partner leaves you without saying a word, it's not the universe punishing you for being a bad person.

Sometimes, shit happens. It sucks; it's painful. But you have options for how you deal with this burden—options more concrete than, "Be a better person and hope the universe rewards you for it." You have a choice to either face the journey ahead of you or bury your head in the sand and retreat within yourself. **And here's another truth: the only way through it...is through it.**

This revelation recently occurred to me without warning. My mother, at 75 years old and in otherwise perfect health (she even looked 20 years younger than her age), all of a sudden had a seizure. The doctors found the worst kind of tumor in her brain. The surprise my family felt was numbing; we had been so comforted by her claims that she was going to live to 104 years old. Given how strong and determined she'd always been—a person who has kept up with all that life has thrown at her for over 75 years—it was easy to believe.

There are no words to express the sadness my dad and I felt during this time. I kept asking, "How did this happen? Why her?" Faced with pain, our minds naturally want to find reason and assign fault. We think in contrasts: right versus wrong, good versus bad. Our minds want to categorize painful experiences to make them easier to feel, manage, and process. If we can't do this, we end up suppressing or numbing our response by acting out, developing addictions, or shutting down that part of us.

I did this with my mom's diagnosis. At first, I was in so much shock that I was completely in denial. I kept thinking, "This can't be true." In the end, I had to tell some of my closest friends, which helped to ground me. By recognizing reality, I felt more present in my body. I was able to connect myself to the current situation. It was painful, but it prevented me from wanting to shut down.

Throughout this time, I was confronted with the expression of "bad things happen to good people." My mom asked the doctors if she had done anything to cause the tumor, but they told her no, nothing; it was a case of bad luck. Sometimes there is no reason; shit just happens. Knowing that, it is important to sit with feelings of sadness and anger that come with unavoidable and unwanted events. After her diagnosis, my mom spent time in deep self-reflection and meditation. She conducted inner guided meditations to talk with the tumor. She chose love and to live fully in each moment. It brought a closeness to my parents' marriage that my dad said they hadn't felt since their early years together, in the mountains of California.

The sweetness that I witnessed between my parents during this difficult time was heart-opening. I processed the pain by reflecting on my own life. I still had my immediate family—my husband and two sons—who were living full lives with their own mini-crises and successes. I focused on my sons and told them they can be deeply saddened by their Nani's health situation *and* feel the joys of their education and girlfriends; both can be true at once.

This balance of holding opposing feelings simultaneously is such a big part of living. It is about having compassion for yourself and legitimizing your feelings while slowing down enough to recognize them. We have to feel everything to travel through those emotions; that is the process of life. Even as a therapist of 25 years, I have to remind myself to pause, be in the moment, *feel* the moment, self-reflect on that feeling, breathe. By avoiding the temptation to suppress our emotions, we allow ourselves to both be and to learn from being.

When you feel sad, allow yourself to *feel* the emotion—don't shy away from it. When you feel anger, express it. When you have a moment of joy or success, stop and celebrate. You deserve good feelings, even (or especially) in the midst of bad feelings. What you don't want is to get stuck in one emotion. If you suppress negative emotions, they will come back to bite at another time. **All emotions are energy, and energy cannot remain inactive.** Your feelings will continue to move inside you and around you until you act them out, at others or yourself, consciously or unconsciously. Learn to be with your emotions, good and bad. They are a part of you and a part of this journey.

Once we begin looking at those events of our lives which hold our disappointments and our pain, our focus needs to be on the emotions trapping us in this stage. We tend to get lost in our own stories—specifically, the ones we have built up in our heads, narratives of pain which cause us to lose sight of our goals and keep us stuck in a cycle of disappointment. How we tell this story (whether to someone else or to ourselves) is dependent upon which emotional state we are in and/or the overarching emotion we feel in relation to the event. It is important to remain focused so that the processing of emotions can lead to trans-forming and healing our disappointments, rather than elaborating on the current story to keep us mired in the past.

In the next chapter, we'll explore what it means to objectively process our feelings of disappointment, pinpointing obstacles and opportunities for healing. This is rarely an easy process, but identifying these obstacles is a necessary first step before planning a path forward.

CHAPTER 2

PROCESSING PAIN

WHEN PROCESSING GRIEF AND disappointment, we experience a wide range of different emotions. These do not occur at random; I consider these emotional responses "stages" that we must each travel through in order to transform and heal. If we don't properly process a stage, we can get stuck in it, endlessly looping through the same moments of drama and/or trauma. A hot-tempered person who always presents an air of contempt during otherwise mundane actions, for example, is probably stuck in a stage of anger or even sadness, i.e., they default to anger to protect that deep vulnerability.

Everyone approaches these stages in their own way and will spend time with each emotion in varying lengths, each to their own comfort level. This is also affected by the severity of the disappointment being processed. Your car being totaled in an accident and the loss of a parent are both upsetting events that would impact your life in a significant way, although one is obviously much more severe. Depending on your childhood experiences, you will have a different "go-to" approach to each emotion in your journey of disappointment. Your pre-established story will influence what you will hold onto and what you will release.

Disappointment and Acceptance

The emotions we feel while moving through disappointment include shock, denial, anger, wishful thinking, depression, bargaining, sadness, and acceptance (wonder), eventually leading to being "at peace" with the event. **The ultimate goal is acceptance, a broad term that represents being free from any harmful beliefs in relation to the disappointment.** There will never be a time when the experience is altogether erased—that is why the objective is to form a "non-attachment" with the situation. Moving beyond the event (or the emotions caused by the event) is a way of unburdening yourself, setting yourself free from any associated negative beliefs that we feel are directly attributed to this negative event.

In fact, part of acceptance is acknowledging that you may still hurt at times. The loss of a parent, child, or spouse results in a profound sadness that ebbs and flows. It is expected for one to be sad, but it is also crucial to move forward from the loss with time. The intention is to reach a state where we smile fondly when we sit with the memories of our loved ones, not one where we perpetually wallow in grief. While we may always miss them, we *can* learn to celebrate the time that we shared with them rather than dwelling on their absence.

There is no other way through the stages of disappointment and grief than to feel the emotions. Only through intimate knowledge of each emotion can we fully understand them; only with a complete understanding can we experience growth. Sometimes we spend an hour with a certain emotion; other times we may spend an entire year with it. We can even bounce wildly between different feelings within a single day. The map to acceptance is different for everyone; it is drawn anew for each individual, customized based on their own wiring and personality.

Depending on the emotion, you may need to spend additional time healing if doing so brings up certain beliefs or triggering memories. You can't simply put aside past or related traumas and say, "Hold on a moment, I'm dealing with *this* right now." In between each stage, there are many opportunities to feel anger, sadness, shock, acceptance... The process is not straightforward. However, using mindfulness tools to move through the stages of disappointment will allow you to continually self-reflect during the experience so that you can transform any given emotion and viewpoint at any given time.

No matter your approach, don't feel frustrated by the pace at which you travel through the healing process. The most important part is that you keep moving in some form. Progress is not measured in distance traveled nor speed maintained; it's measured in direction—forward. Stagnancy in a pond can create unsafe algae; think of your inner self the same way. If we avoid confronting our emotions—anger, sadness, even acceptance (if there is guilt associated with the idea of "moving on," also known as **survivor's guilt**)—we are only giving ourselves permission to remain stuck. Like stagnant water, that stillness only invites toxins into our system.

Sadly, many spend their entire lifetime stuck in a stage or emotion. It's not their fault: our minds developed to try and make sense of the happenings around us. We are constantly asking ourselves questions like, "Is this good or bad?" or "Is this safe or dangerous?" These thoughts activate our **amygdala**, triggering the fight-or-flight response through the release of stress hormones. This basic, primal response exists within us only to keep us safe; it doesn't care whether we are happy, just that we're alive. Maybe that was fine for our hunter-gatherer ancestors, but modern attachments mean we can often get tripped up by this primitive response.

Sometimes it helps to have a goal in mind before you start your healing journey. This will vary from person to person, based on the event, pain endured, and life history leading up to the disappointment. It is good to have something to work towards because you are less likely to get stuck. With that said, it is still important to exist fully in the moment of whichever emotion you are currently processing. Be present with each stage and don't try to rush ahead; just be open to embracing the potential of a transformational resolution, one that you can actively work towards.

I invite you to establish a specific objective that inspires you to keep moving forward. You do not want to feel hijacked by the event and any subsequent beliefs born from it. The gifts you were born with will help you confront and process these emotions, but you will also need courage to look at and respond to all of them on a deeper level.

WORKSHOP

Look at the list of painful or disappointing memories you wrote for the previous workshop. Pick one that you would like further insight into and to change the narrative around.

- What part of this event is the most painful? What stands out the most to you?

- What part of this event is factual?

- What part of this event is (your) interpretation?

The lens in which you view your trauma–the facts versus the interpretations–influences how you handle the trauma. If you can recognize a theme to your lens, this is a good place to start; you will know exactly what to address. Being able to figure out what part of your healing journey you want to focus on is important because it helps prevent you from going around in circles. We can often get caught in a loop of our story and associated pain. Similar to spreading out puzzle pieces to organize them first, breaking down the trauma and looking at the parts individually helps you see the bigger picture. It brings more clarity to the situation.

(continued next page)

Some overcome disappointment faster or easier than others. You may have noticed in your own life that you are slower to reach acceptance after a difficult experience. If this is true for you, know that this is not a flaw. **Don't make the recovery process a competition between yourself and others.** It is a deeply personal experience that we all approach in our own, unique way.

Disappointment and Resilience

Being resilient in times of hardship has to do with our ability to stay strong and remain present in the face of adversity, drawing on our sources of inner vitality to sustain us during our struggles. This ability differs from person to person in each of its aspects: physical, emotional, and spiritual. For example, someone may be able to endure physical pain but find lingering emotional trauma stifling. We all have different tolerance levels. Our "superpower" of positive self-esteem plays a big role in our resilience reserves; we'll explore means of strengthening this in Chapter 4.

In the second half of this book, you will have the opportunity to travel through the stages of disappointment at your own speed. I will help to guide you through it, but the choice to take each step—whether a day at a time or a week at a time—will be your own. Everyone dances to the beat differently; the important thing is to hear the song in its entirety. I encourage you to contemplate each lesson carefully, which is to say, live in and experience each emotion with mindfulness and courage. In doing so, you learn to be more present and aware in general.

We also can't skip any stages because that would mean avoiding or ignoring an emotion. **When we are grieving, we need to feel.** That can be a scary prospect; we fear we will get stuck in or overcome by the emotion, or we are simply afraid to confront that particular emotion and experience what it brings up. Being resilient means being able to handle these emotions. Have a conversation about these feelings with yourself so that you can realign how you view the disappointment and the story connected to it. Ultimately, this enables us to let go of the morbid stories that haunt us.

With hard work, I believe that we all have the capability to heal the old pains of the past. We can all reach our own personalized idea of "peace." Remember: it isn't what happened to you but how you make sense of it. You, too, can learn how to live with the experience so that it no longer has power over you and your life.

WORKSHOP

Resilience is the ability to keep up, to endure—whether in a relationship, at a job, with a hobby, etc. We all have an energy force within us, known as vitality, that acts as fuel for our resiliency. The more vitality we have, the stronger our ability to sit with disappointment, make changes as needed, and eventually evolve from the disappointing experience.

Drama and trauma can impact our resilience and, by extension, our vitality. By working on our whole self—body, mind, and spirit—we strengthen these two attributes. Here are some tools to help exercise your resilience and vitality.

Yoga

There are many different kinds of yoga. Find one that speaks to you. This is a personal choice, so choosing a method that you connect with is important. You'll want to enjoy it so that you are happy enough to commit to daily practice.

(continued next page)

Meditation

Meditation takes many forms: some focus on breathwork and/or chanting, while others ask you to sit in silence. Some are more physical, requiring you to hold *asana* (body postures) and *mudra* (hand gestures) as you practice. I personally love breathwork and chanting-based meditations. If you enjoy meditations as a mental health and life tool, you can find over 60 meditations and audios on my website (MadhurNain.com).

Prayer

If you are religious (and doing so doesn't trigger additional negative emotions), find some hymns or prayers from your denomination that call to you. Write them down and keep them on your bedside table. Recite them daily until you know them by heart.

Dance

Move your body regularly. Incorporating vocal music into this movement is especially helpful—especially if you join in with the vocalization. By singing, you unite your body, mind, and spirit even more.

Connect with Nature

Try a hobby that you can enjoy outdoors, like hiking, gardening, or swimming. This will help you connect to the earth.

Bodywork

There are many practitioners who do bodywork, such as massages (soft tissue) and energy work (*reiki*). If you do not notice any benefits, either try someone new (sometimes it might be a matter of the wrong practitioner) or move on and look for something else that works for you. This is a personal preference, not a one-size-fits-all situation, so listen to your body's needs.

(continued next page)

Exercise and Good Nutrition

People often rely on exercise to maintain good physical health, but nutrition is equally important. Be conscious about what you put into your body and maintain good eating habits. Your diet should predominantly consist of whole foods.

Let's pause a moment to reflect. You have now made a list of events that are painful for you, which keep showing up in your life and limiting your growth potential. You have broken down these events in a way that allows you to see them for what they are—trauma and triggers. Moving forward, your focus is to process these events with an objective of healing from them.

It may seem daunting to view them all at once but worry not: **you have vitality on your side, an internal energy source that supports your healing so that you can do the work.** And that's not all—vitality is just one part of the innate power we each hold inside. Locating and understanding our gifts—most notably, the real-life superpower of self-esteem—is the next important step in processing grief.

It can be a challenge all its own to accept your strengths when you've spent so long dwelling on perceived weaknesses. In the next chapter, I'll help you learn to first identify, and then acknowledge, the amazing abilities you already possess that will support you during this journey. By learning about your innate gifts, you will dive deeper into learning more about yourself. You will learn how to use those gifts—and, ultimately, learn to recognize that you are special in your own way *because* of those gifts.

CHAPTER 3

ACKNOWLEDGING YOUR INNATE GIFTS

W E ARE ALL UNIQUE. As different as individual fingerprints, we each have our own personalities and our own deep inner beliefs which determine how we approach life. These innate qualities impact how we see the world, and they influence how we deal with everything life throws at us. **In other words, how we react and respond to disappointments is a direct result of our inherent wiring.** Because of this, no two people will experience disappointment in the same way.

Processing pain and trauma is something we learn and practice throughout life. Unfortunately, we don't always learn to process trauma properly, often leading to a reliance on bad habits as unhealthy emotional responses. When we are unable to handle disappointments gracefully, it can be frustrating and consequently feel like a shortcoming. This can be further exacerbated by fostering shortsightedness, as we question our own ability to confront any given situation. We go from actively confronting disappointment to setting ourselves up as the victim, miring ourselves in a rut of self-defeating thoughts or the false belief that it is always someone else's fault.

This is why learning how to properly self-reflect is so important.

Within our unique selves, we all have built-in tools—our character traits—that can help us navigate through and overcome obstacles, as long as we understand their proper use. You may have noticed how some of us shut down when confronted with a difficult situation, while others approach difficulties with more tenacity. This doesn't mean that the tenacious individuals are immune to emotional discomfort (in fact, it might mean that they don't feel as detached as they could when something doesn't follow their expectations). What it means is that they have better command of their individual tools when it comes to dealing with disappointment. Upon being confronted with pain, we all have the ability to process it in our own, distinct way. It is a matter of locating that tool, honing it, and applying it. That is your gift, even if you don't know it yet.

If you are not yet convinced that you have this potential within you, it is never "too late" to discover it. **There is always time and opportunity for you to strengthen your traits, provided you don't insist on holding yourself back with a negative self-image.** By being empathetic towards yourself, you can reclaim aspects that you previously viewed as shortcomings.

Take me, for example. I have always been a very sensitive person, but I used to wish I wasn't. I wished I didn't care what others thought about me or how they reacted to me. I disliked how I would take interactions so personally; they hurt me and left me feeling alone and sorry for myself. Then I learned to view this perceived shortcoming as a gift, which has since become an essential aspect of my work.

My viewpoint towards my own sensitivity changed as I built up my self-esteem. I started to see myself differently, including my choices about how I responded and reacted to the world at large. This came out of doing my own self-reflective work during the mid-90s, notably with daily meditation and occasionally working with my own psychotherapist. A big part was simply getting older. Maturity can play a role in self-growth; it allows us to tap into an inner awareness that we can "let stuff go." When we are younger, we tend to hold onto our beliefs. In my own work, I learned about the strength of blessing the situation, including any person(s) involved, and leaned into the power of letting go.

As a psychotherapist, I must be able to understand my clients from both an objective and subjective standpoint. I aim to not only be a witness to their experience but to also feel it with them in a healthy way. Since we are not all wired the same way, it can be difficult for some clients to tell me exactly how they feel; on the flip side, telling someone exactly how to deal with any specific situation will always be a tricky business. This is when it helps to be a sensitive, perceptive, responsive individual. The positive side of sensitivity is intuitive sense. I now embrace that sensitivity is my superpower.

Being willing and able to do something as simple as asking others how they are (and truly listening to their answer) lets me build a deeper relationship and connection with them. If I can understand the uniqueness of another person, then I can do more than witness their pain and suffering. I begin to truly see them on a soul level. If I wasn't such a sensitive person, I would not be able to do this. I don't think I could do my job as well as I need to. This quality—one I initially viewed as a negative trait—has evolved into a tool I now cherish.

WORKSHOP

It is time for your "Wise Self" to take a stand. Your Wise Self is who you are at this exact age, with all the learned experiences and knowledge of life thus far. The Wise Self is curious, open, present, and kind. It is here to protect you by holding boundaries in place and preventing outer reactions to cause inner triggers. Through the Wise Self, you learn that you don't need to take everything personally. Think, then act.

Releasing yourself from the burdens of disappointment takes courage and trust for oneself. Only you can manifest these qualities. Find the strength to address negative thoughts by writing them down on a piece of paper for your Wise Self to process. Negative self-talk can be a barrier to recognizing your unique self and your gifts, which can also create a roadblock on your healing journey. Instead, open up the dialogue with yourself. Let's start with some questions:

- What makes you unique? How do you differ from your family, friends, and/or coworkers?

- List some of your positive personality traits. How have these traits impacted your life? Name some of your shortcomings. How have these shortcomings impacted your life?

- Why do you feel these are shortcomings? How can you turn them into positive traits?

- If you could change something about your traits and/or shortcomings, what would you change? Why? How could this benefit you?

- How can your character traits help carry you through moments of disappointment?

Shift Self-Perception with Self-Introspection

"How are you feeling?"

It seems like a simple question. When I work with couples, I will often pose this question after someone has disclosed something personal and intense. Sometimes I will ask if they feel closer, more distant, or numb. This creates an opening for a more intimate, honest conversation. By distilling the moment, it asks for the listener(s) to be present and in their body.

How we ask questions and how we listen can impact our openness with others—and even ourselves. Feeling close means feeling connected, which can amplify the powers of compassion.

It is equally important to extend this curiosity to yourself by checking in on your own well-being. Asking yourself how you are feeling builds a deeper relationship and connection with yourself. Think of it as holding an internal conversation. Take some advice from a sensitive person and be empathetic towards yourself.

This level of introspection may not come naturally, depending on individual differences. How we were raised also plays a role, in that it influences the degree to which our unique gifts are cultivated or suppressed. It's like a piece of sharp glass that gets tumbled by lapping ocean waves, becoming smooth over time. Loving, supportive parents can provide this sort of polishing. Raising my two sons, I focused on giving them the space and opportunity to grow. I tried to recognize their gifts and help them expand upon those traits. Having been empowered at a young age, they now have a better mental capacity to navigate through their life's journey and all that it entails.

This is not to say that I have been (or currently am) a perfect parent. I have made mistakes, and I am sure I will continue to stumble occasionally. What matters is that I continue to live with the focus of being a healthy parent for my two sons, no matter what. The power of self-reflection is the power to learn and grow from our mistakes—a privilege that we all have.

Yet not everyone is so lucky; without this type of supportive upbringing, our gifts may go unrecognized or unpolished or fail us in a time of need. Not every child has the same support system that my sons have enjoyed. Even with my loving parents, I did not have this myself. When we lack that support, it can feel quite isolating and cause us to question our abilities. This is especially dangerous once we start confronting hardships. If we have not carefully cultivated our gifts, a hidden part of our personality—such as anxiety, OCD, and depression—can emerge during moments of grief. These qualities can be a hindrance as we try to connect to ourselves, further deepening our disconnect.

Our unique qualities shape how we look at, relate to, and try to make sense of disappointment, grief, and pain. When we can't connect to our individualistic strengths, the journey of moving past disappointments becomes that much more difficult and can last a lot longer. Have you seen a person live completely immersed in their pain or trauma, almost as if they cannot let it go? It ends up shaping and controlling much of their life.

It isn't always easy to shift away from an identity formed during childhood. We are often locked into the ideas projected onto us by our parental figures, as well as childhood experiences that shaped our expectations. It is worth considering our own neurotic thinking and/or behaviors, as acknowledging them can encourage the mind to do better. Confronted with an undesirable reality, we are inspired to stop, evaluate, and adjust.

It might feel hard, frustrating, or unfair to complete this sort of self-inventory, but the ability to self-reflect is essential: it helps us to identify the good and the bad, determine what can remain and what needs to change, and gives us the wherewithal to execute those necessary actions. **The goal is to grow.** Throughout my undergraduate studies, I used to say, "Every day, I become a little less stupider." Poor grammar, yes, but that is precisely the point: we are never "perfect." We are always growing, even if the process is slow. We never stop this process, not until our last breath.

WORKSHOP

Travel back to your childhood by thinking of a specific memory in which you felt disappointment. Write down your answers as you process the following questions:

- What was the event that disappointed you? How old were you?

- At that age, what was the overarching view/expectation you had about your life?

- How is that view/expectation different now from when you were younger?

- While you were dealing with the disappointment in this memory, did you notice other people reacting or responding differently? How did they behave?

- If you did not notice others reacting/responding differently, is it because your disappointment was so strong that all you could think about was your own experience? How could it have helped if you did acknowledge others' behaviors?

- Think about how it would feel if you had approached this disappointment with a more neutral perspective. What would it feel like? Would your mindset change? Why, or why not?

Innate Challenges

Eastern philosophy—including yogic teachings—suggests that each person is born with their own *karma*. This does not mean someone is born good or evil, nor does it mean a person's fate is unchangeable. Rather, *karma* explains that each person is born with a soul, and that soul is meant to work on certain lessons in this lifetime.

Have you ever noticed the same issue appearing over and over in your life? This may be the universe's way of calling you to action, or it may be a sign that some aspect of your self encourages or attracts these problems. In either case, you have two choices: you can either get upset at the reoccurring issue, or you can stop to ask yourself, "Why does this keep happening? What am I missing? What can I do differently to learn from this? How can I react differently to change the outcome?"

My mom has a great saying: "Life without crisis is life in a coffin." Crises are life's puzzles; solving them is a brain exercise that allows our capacity for cognitive and emotional awareness to expand. Because we are constantly troubleshooting these issues derived from disappointment, we are in a continual state of transformation and growth. It can be challenging or even exhausting at times, but each puzzle we solve is another chance at refining the lens through which we look at life.

Within my own life, I know that I still have work to do. Even if I now view my sensitive nature as a positive trait in my professional life, it requires maintenance to prevent it from disrupting my personal relationships. To achieve this, I am in constant conversation with myself through daily meditation and talks with my inner parts (specifically, the young girl inside me). Quiet introspection allows me to view myself and my feelings on a neutral plane so that I can process my life openly and honestly—as well as with self-love and compassion.

It is important to be kind to yourself, especially as you are self-evaluating. You need a safe space to operate, one which offers forgiveness for any perceived weaknesses. For me, I want to avoid getting upset over my relationships with others and their relationships with me. For example, when I think of my sons who have started to pull away as they become men, it hurts. But I also understand it is supposed to happen. I can't take their growth personally. It takes work to remind myself that they are maturing through a natural process, but it's work well worth doing. When I put my own sensitivities aside, I can even cherish this process. I recognize that I am actively experiencing my own mental growth as I watch my sons mature into strong, independent, and loving men building their own lives.

When life becomes an active experience for us, we are better able to trust that situations can change. This epiphany should come as a wonderful relief. When we feel as though we can safely *be* with certain variables of life, we learn to fully exist in the moment. With this empowerment, we become more relaxed with the process of life. We all have this ability; we just need the proper training and tools to bring it out. All it takes is practice and patience.

Meditation can help train our minds into reaching a state of consciousness and unattachment. The more self-aware we are, the more we can work on our "Soul Self," the part of our being that most reflects our essential qualities. If we are blind to our inherent nature, especially any negative personality traits, then we cannot address them and enhance or transform them (as needed). **By self-reflecting, we can better connect to our identity.**

When we connect to our Soul Self, we learn to embrace the process and function with impartiality. Being connected to our Soul Self means having our mind, heart, and body be so perfectly aligned that we move *with* the flow of life. By leaning into the experience around us, we let go of our attachments to specific outcomes. We still have wants and desires, of course, but we are less likely to be reactive if they don't work out. This allows us to deal with hardships with grace, which strengthens our Wise Self. We can reduce the impact of disappointment by being with it: directly confronting and actively processing it.

Our unique qualities each affect the meaning we give to the pain in our lives. By acknowledging our uniqueness—our gifts and our shortcomings, our positive and negative traits—we have a better understanding of our disposition and how to approach grief. We are better able to distance ourselves so that we can respond, rather than react, to situations with a clear mind. It gives us the space to be detached in our observations and surrender ourselves to the outcome. It gives us self-confidence, which enables us to temper our feelings of disappointment.

It will take work to build up this self-assuredness, but be patient with yourself. You will eventually have the courage and compassion needed to be with yourself as you ride the waves of disappointment and heal yourself by processing the various emotions related to the event.

Creative Outlets: Expressing Your Emotions

We can build our self-esteem by practicing different modes of self-reflection. This can happen through journaling, meditation, and other hobbies (like creating art). Make a commitment to yourself to practice one of these modes regularly and hold yourself to this commitment.

For example, research has shown that journaling supports your mental health as you work through your feelings. Set a timer for 10 minutes and write what you notice within yourself: thoughts, feelings, images, events. It doesn't need to make sense, and don't worry about spelling or grammar—just get the words down. (I have dyslexia, so this advice helped me to get over my self-judgment.)

Your journal is for you, and no one else—it is a safe space to express yourself in whatever capacity you want. If you're worried about your words being read by someone else, find a journal that has a lock and key so that no one will be able to access it but you. And while studies have shown that writing by hand creates a change in the brain structure and supports mental health, you can use a computer if it is easier for you. For privacy, you can password protect your files. Doing the journaling is more important than doing it "right," as that will differ per individual and their needs/wants anyway.

Journaling has many other benefits outside of generally being a creative outlet. It can reduce anxiety, support you when you are brooding, sharpen your awareness and perception of life, and encourage you to be more open and present. By writing your words down, you are required to really look at your thoughts and feelings. This can help you to regulate your emotions. Once you acknowledge and understand your emotions, you can choose to change them if you want. Journaling while moving through disappointment is a great way to support your transition from emotion to emotion as you move towards acceptance and peace.

If journaling is not your forte, try a different endeavor. Think of hobbies you have currently and expand upon them. You could even revisit certain hobbies you've had in the past. Hobbies help you to feel good about yourself through positive creative outlets. If nothing else, make a list of things you loved to do as a child or wished you had tried as a child. Pick one at a time and try practicing it routinely for three weeks to three months.

You can also supplement any of these activities with meditation. Commit to practicing for three minutes daily for two weeks. If you enjoy it, work up to a daily practice for three months. If you have trouble meditating or don't know how to start, visit my website (MadhurNain. com) or check out my other book (*The Stressless Brain*) which contains 26 meditations including instructions and music downloads. There are also some free meditation downloads provided with this book.

CHAPTER 4

SELF-ESTEEM:
A Hidden Superpower

HOW YOU FEEL ABOUT yourself is a huge factor in your ability to self-heal. Our self-esteem is directly affected by our experiences, which include pain and trauma. **If you feel bad about yourself—whether part of a longstanding narrative or as a gut reaction inspired by your circumstances—everything becomes more difficult.** Self-reflection becomes a struggle, making it harder to grieve and let go. You may even find yourself wallowing in defeat instead of counteracting it.

How does this happen? For starters, our childhood experiences create internalized expectations of ourselves. When we are still learning about how the world works, we test boundaries; we experiment, we act out. This exploration is a perfectly normal part of our development.

How our parents react to this boundary-pushing stage, however, is what directly influences our personalities—and our self-esteem—as adults. Depending on how much they celebrated or criticized your gifts and shortcomings, they may have either inflated or deflated your sense of self-worth.

When my boys were young and misbehaving, I would make a point to specify that it was their *actions* that were the issue—not them. It is an important distinction to make, albeit a difficult one to appreciate at that age. In fact, when my younger son was in his teens, he once chided me during a discussion by sarcastically noting, "I know, mom. It's not me; it's my behavior."

I made sure to offer my sons love and support (within certain boundaries), unaffected by their behavior at any given time. But I also encouraged them to behave in ways that would benefit their personal relationships and create harmony for society at large. By setting the boundaries of what is and isn't acceptable at a young age, a child is allowed to find out who they are in a secure setting. As they mature, the boundaries expand, and they are given more room to explore; but they will do so along the same patterns of safe experimentation that they followed in their youth. They are able to be more secure in their actions because they have the support of unconditional, nonjudgmental love from the parent. Because they had the support from their parent, a child is then able to place the utmost faith in the processes and outcomes of life.

When we receive a negative message from our caretakers—be it our parents, or whoever may have raised us—we can feel bad about our identity and who we are. Shame and guilt can lower our morale. These emotions are often established within us at young ages, in our most formative years. If we are berated after an accident, we'll download that negative reaction into our system, where it remains a core component of our personality for years to come.

WORKSHOP

Think about the kinds of messages you received about your self-worth as a child, both positive and negative. Write some of these messages down, noting the (approximate) age you were when you started to hear them.

- What was your self-esteem like as a child? How has this manifested itself in adulthood?

- In your childhood, what was the message you received from your parental figure(s) about you and your ability to do things?

- What other caretakers—aside from your parental figure(s)—had a big influence on your self-esteem? (This could be anyone, from a teacher or coach to another family member.) How did they treat your gifts and/or shortcomings? What did you think of their opinion of you?

- How do you feel about yourself? Are you critical of yourself? Do you easily get defensive? Do you shut others out or cut others off if they call you out on your behavior?

- What are things about yourself that feel good?

We can and must build our up own self-esteem throughout the course of our life. This represents an ongoing process, an investment in our own well-being. We make these investments by actively practicing self-love and espousing a positive regard for our self. But self-care is difficult for many. This is why not everyone you meet has healthy self-esteem; I would even go so far as to say that *most* people don't have healthy self-esteem or self-worth. Rather than being generated naturally, self-esteem is a direct result of self-care, a mark of the amount of work you've put into building yourself up.

There are certain tools, activities, and ways of thinking that support building healthy self-esteem. However, it is important to acknowledge that there is no magic pill that instantly instills confidence. **The same way physical exercise influences external change, internal change comes from daily action on your part.** You will need to build *and* maintain the quality of self-worth within yourself. It will take time. It is not a sudden experience of, "Oh, I love myself now! All is okay." It is something you must continually practice while traveling through the ups and downs of life.

So, where to begin? First of all, strive to treat yourself with kindness—mentally, physically, emotionally, and spiritually. Kindness goes a long way. What are some kind things you can do or say to yourself daily? Weekly? This can be anything from eating healthier to thinking and/or speaking positive affirmations to yourself. Gratitude journaling is another great option and can be incredibly helpful because it requires focusing on the good. Start by listing three things that you are thankful for each day, working your way up to listing ten things daily. It can be as simple as, "I am grateful that I don't have to worry about filling up my car with gas," or even, "The cup of coffee I had today was especially yummy, and I enjoyed it."

Meditation and/or affirmations to build self-esteem can be utilized throughout the day. Try this little routine: every morning, say a positive affirmation ten times (once with each finger) and repeat the practice at the end of the day. During the day, whenever you say or have a negative thought about yourself, say your positive affirmation. This helps to rewire negative, self-deprecating thought patterns you have about yourself by changing them to something positive instead.

Sometimes it helps to have a **mantra**—a repeated statement or sound that aids in concentration—as you navigate through your responses to other people and events in your life. For me, I often think of the old saying, "I am the grace of God." I would say this out loud, take a deep breath, and say it again. By repeating a mantra or affirmation in such a way, we allow ourselves to stop in the moment and shift our behavior and way of thinking. Each person can find an affirmation that works for them, and each person can apply it in a way that prevents them from mentally spiraling. This mantra can be anything that is positive about yourself but not above all else or others.

You can use any mantra or positive affirmation, or you could even make up your own. The most important part is that you use it.

If you're looking for somewhere to start, here are some mantra and affirmations which I have used to build up my self-esteem and keep it healthy:

- "Humee Hum Braham Hum"

- Serenity prayer

- "I Matter" meditation

- "I am a glorious, gracious, child of God. I am joyful, serene, positive, and loving."

Other ways to build self-esteem include different hobbies, like painting, playing an instrument, and/or getting involved in a sport. When we are active in doing things that bring happiness and fulfillment to our lives, it helps make us feel competent and satisfied. We don't even have to be good at the activity, especially at first, so long as we find some sense of joy and accomplishment from it. In the end, it is about devoting time to do something that is for yourself.

These are just some examples of ways to be active in your building of self-esteem. The most important thing is that you actually commit to practicing these self-care activities regularly, if not daily. It takes 10,000 hours to master something. So, if you want to master feeling good about and with yourself, then you need to put in the time and do it!

Many of us have negative thought patterns regarding our self-esteem or self-worth. They pop up at different times in our life, often triggered from something happening around us. This is normal. Again, we need to learn what these patterns are so that we can change them. The more we understand our negative self-talk, the easier we can pinpoint what areas of our self-esteem we need to work on. It can be about our body, our self-image (how we see ourselves or how we perceive others seeing us), or how we think about ourselves. Let's do a little workshop to find out more about these patterns.

WORKSHOP

Many of us have negative thought patterns regarding our self-esteem or self-worth. They pop up at different times in our life, often triggered from something happening around us. This is normal. Again, we need to learn what these patterns are so that we can change them. The more we understand our negative self-talk, the easier we can pinpoint what areas of our self-esteem we need to work on. It can be about our body, our self-image (how we see ourselves or how we perceive others seeing us), or how we think about ourselves.

(continued next page)

Let's find out more about these patterns. Think about a time when you made a mistake or reacted poorly to a situation, then answer the following questions. Repeat this for several other times when you made a mistake or reacted poorly to a situation, then compare your answers. Do you see a pattern repeated? How might you break these patterns in the future?

- How did you feel about yourself and your behavior after this event?

- Did someone call you out on this mistake? If so, how did you react to them? Did you internalize this reaction, or did you confront the other person? Why did you react this way?

- Did you view yourself as a bad person because you made this mistake? Why or why not?

- How could you have approached the situation differently to avoid a negative response?

Defensiveness: Embracing Critique to Avoid Conflict

Self-esteem plays a crucial role in our ability to heal and move past disappointment because it provides a reservoir of healthy self-value that can be drawn upon when encountering triggering memories and emotions. This is not a matter of feeling better than those around you. Rather, this is a mindset that establishes that we are all of equal value. It demands that we are all deserving of respect, including yourself—from yourself.

The ways in which we react to adverse conditions and confrontations are related to our self-esteem. A knee-jerk negative reaction to someone calling us out on our issues, for example, is an internal defense mechanism designed to avoid true self-reflection. When self-reflection is viewed as potentially uncomfortable, it only makes sense to come up with methods of avoidance, unhealthy and unhelpful though they may be.

Defensiveness kicks in when our amygdala is activated into a fight, flight, freeze, or fix response. It is a natural human reaction to many situations; however, unless it is properly regulated, it cannot serve its original primal purpose. Left unchecked, being overly defensive takes us out of our awareness (also known as **secondary consciousness**) and causes us to be more reactive. This will create conflict every time.

You may be wondering, "What exactly is self-esteem? How do I differentiate it from being confident or cocky?" There are plenty of people out in the world with an inflated sense of importance. (You see this a lot on social media, in particular.) **The big difference is how one responds to constructive criticism.** This should not be confused with negative criticism, as "constructive" is exactly that: something which aids growth potential.

Those who are around us a lot will see all sides of us, good and bad. They are often able to observe parts of us that we have a hard time seeing ourselves. When we are self-assured, we are secure when hearing constructive criticism. We have the emotional maturity to listen, learn, and grow. As I mentioned before, life is a journey of growth—and transformation.

If someone you love and trust says something about you or your behavior, it is in your best interest to pause and reflect on it. What happens next depends on our self-esteem. When we have healthy self-esteem, we are able to stop and consider: "Is there any truth in what they are saying?" If we find there *is* truth in their statement, healthy self-esteem gives us the ability to say, "Thank you. I will work on this," or "Can you help me understand what you mean? Can you give me some examples of when I do this?" (Of course, if what they are saying is not true, you don't need to do or say anything. That is why it is helpful to inquire.) This ability to refrain from taking the bait can *only* be done when we have healthy self-esteem. It is a complex emotional juggling act, but it is one that anyone can learn and master—with time, practice, and patience.

That said, most of us will have some kind of reaction when someone calls us out on something in a way that sounds or feels like negative criticism. It is important to differentiate whether the intention of the critique is genuine. When my sons pointed out my unfavorable behavior, I would wonder, "Is there any truth in what they are saying?" If there was, I knew I needed to adjust. If what they were saying was not true, I knew I needed to keep in mind that they were just reacting to the situation, which did *not* give me an excuse to "double down." What matters is responding to the call to pause and reevaluate. The willingness to do so counters the negative inclination towards defensiveness.

A major component in this self-evaluation is to disengage from taking words personally. Be careful not to take reactions at face value, especially when they are shared during heated conversations. Rather than having a back-and-forth argument, remain rational and responsive. Once both parties are calm and level, try to talk things through again.

As you parse through constructive criticism, be mindful and connected to your feelings. As the saying goes, "Be curious, not judgmental." That goes for yourself and those others who have your best interests at heart. Individuals communicating clearly, thoughtfully, and with love *do* want to help you. When we have a healthy grasp of our ego, we are able to exist comfortably in our self-worth. We do not fly off the handles when faced with feedback from others. We feel secure enough to assess their words, without feeling threatened. If their feedback isn't true, there's no need to overreact; you can simply let it go. If their feedback is true, have enough self-assurance to take on the critique and apply it.

Terry Real, a family therapist, is no stranger to this viewpoint. As an author, he has talked about "joining through the truth" with couples. When we are able to sit in healthy confidence with ourselves, we can extend the same courtesy to others in our life. By being honest with yourself, you are able to both give and receive counsel without resentment. You can function with impartiality to your own behavior, as well as others' needs and wants.

So, defining healthy self-esteem is simple: it refers to when we're operating with confidence and compassion. We love ourselves, acknowledge our flaws (by working on them), and celebrate our strengths. With self-esteem, we are formidable. It gives us the drive and focus to be our own hero by kicking down the door of disappointment and saving ourselves in the process.

Sometimes, a Superhero Needs a Sidekick

When we feel good about ourselves, it's easier to resist getting dragged down by residual pain from past disappointment. As you progress through the stages of disappointment, you will find yourself wanting this superpower. But self-reflection—and the healing that comes with it—is hard work; it will push every button within you. Processing the grief that comes with disappointment will become so much easier when you are secure in yourself and your own abilities. Just because you have established a degree of confidence, however, doesn't mean that you always have to be self-assured; it just means that your overarching view is that you believe that you are a good person who sometimes makes mistakes. Terry Real commonly talks about this when discussing the difference between healthy shame and toxic shame.

Healthy shame is when we hold ourselves in high regard. Even when we make a mistake, we still know that we are essentially a good person—both can be true at the same time. **Toxic shame** is when we do something wrong and think we are a bad person as a result. When we are in a state of toxic shame, all it takes is the slightest bit of negative criticism to send us into a downward spiral or to lash out at the other person—even a loving spouse or our own children.

Working on our self-esteem helps us stay in the lane of healthy shame. This can be hard, especially if we had a lot of drama and/or trauma in our childhood. Please, do not feel it is demeaning to reach out if you need help processing these emotions. In fact, I think it is courageous, and I am proud of you for requesting help if you need it.

If you find that you have little to no self-esteem, I highly recommend that you work with a licensed psychotherapist for additional assistance. You may need someone to walk with you as you move through the timeline of disappointment. This book can provide some support, but a therapist that you can trust and feel a connection with is an invaluable tool. They can be a pillar of support for you to lean on as old pains trigger new and old emotions. To find a professional in your area, consider checking PsychologyToday.com.

CHAPTER 5

THROUGH FAITH, THERE IS HOPE

W E'VE DISCUSSED SELF-ESTEEM AND self-reflection, but both of these concepts rely on something deeper: self-knowledge. It is crucial for you to know who you are if you are to heal, change and grow out of your current state. If you are not secure within yourself, then you will not be able to locate or walk down the paths that you are meant to follow. **Knowing yourself is the compass that guides you through the journey.**

In Viktor Frankl's *Man's Search for Meaning* (1946), he quotes philosopher Friedrich Nietzsche: "He who has a 'why' to live for can bear almost any 'how.'" In simpler terms, when you know your purpose in life—your "why"—then you can more easily identify and commit to doing whatever it takes to achieve that purpose—your "how." So many in today's world don't have a "why," beyond nebulous ideas like "being successful"; their achievements are treated like a to-do list of chores that are checked off as they are completed. I don't think that is what Nietzsche was talking about. I believe your "why" should be something more intangible, with a wholesome component to it.

For example, my main "why" is to provide unconditional love to my children. I do not control them or force them to be a certain way or to do certain things. I see them for who they are and support them on their life's journey. But I have another "why," which is extending my love to humanity at large by connecting with other people and their cultures. In other words, my other "why" is about having experiences beyond myself. I feel alive in these moments, which leaves me feeling connected to all. This is in alignment with my inner belief that we are all united, in one way or another. Although your beliefs might differ, I believe there is an energy force which tethers us together—and this energy guides us.

Recognizing that there is a force greater than yourself gives you grace as you undergo the processes of life. My way of thinking proposes that, if we are all connected to a singular source, we are never truly alone. Think about that: if we are all connected, then we all matter equally. Understanding this sentiment builds trust—with yourself and with others—even as the pendulum of life swings back and forth between its many extremes (good and bad, up and down, right and wrong).

When working on healing pain caused by past drama and/or trauma, we may have to look at multiple perspectives for a clear vision of the entire situation. Having a connection to a greater energy gives us an ability to be less attached, which helps us to see different sides. It is not always obvious if there was a "right" side, or whether the events that happened were justified. This is when we have to refocus ourselves on our objective: healing from this pain. What do you want to get out of this traumatic memory? Is it to be right? Happy? To simply move forward? There is no one-size-fits-all answer. This is your journey, after all.

However, even on the shortest trips, we leave prepared. In this life's journey, we are more easily able to let go of our attachments when we have some kind of faith. It helps with letting go of ideations of revenge, where acting out on these thoughts would only hurt us further by tethering us to the cycle of pain. Placing your faith in something larger than yourself helps you forge a connection to your Soul Self, freeing you from attachments like emotions and/or beliefs associated with painful events. These restrictive beliefs are then replaced with a simple faith in the process of life.

Being connected to a source greater than yourself will also help support your self-esteem. Believing in something you can't hear, see, or touch can help give you that connection to the "why." Faith is a humbling experience like that. What is your "why?"

WORKSHOP

Establishing faith, feeling connected to something bigger than yourself... these things do not necessarily happen overnight. Allow this process to take the time it needs to be effective. It is *normal* to be skeptical, especially given the negative perceptions organized religion has created around faith. As someone raised in a yoga-cult community, I have had to find my own path of healing away from the confining doctrines I was taught. I have had to sit and contemplate what the meaning of life, and faith itself, is for me. I invite you to be open and curious about this specific journey—and be kind to yourself if it feels uncomfortable.

- How has religion and/or faith shown up in your life? Was it too much? Was it not enough? Was it absent? Was there betrayal involved with your experience?

- Think about your own faith doctrine before addressing the following questions: Did your parental figure(s) have a "why?" How did you know what it was? How did they live by it? How did it influence you? Was this positive or negative for you?

- What does the prospect of a higher energy or greater source mean to you?

(continued next page)

- What do you believe in that allows you to feel connected?

- How do you not feel alone in life? Do you feel like something or someone has your back? What does this feel like for you?

- Do you have pain in relation to your faith? If so, how have you made sense of this? How has it stunted you? Are you stuck in an emotion around it? Would you like to remove yourself from the pain while maintaining your faith? How do you think this may be possible?

The Faith Doctrine

When you break down most religions, they are very similar in makeup: **the presence of a higher power (one greater than us) calls us to love our fellow human beings, work hard, be kind, and serve others.** A minister—be it a priest, a rabbi, or other holy person—guides us to happiness through scriptures, prayer, song, and other rituals. But while the essence of religion is the same across all cultures, it can often get corrupted by outside influences. Power, money, and prestige can infiltrate faith and shift its purpose.

I come from a long lineage of faith on both sides of my family, including such diverse practices as Kundalini yoga, the Episcopal Church, and Catholicism. While I value the benefits this rich history of faith has provided me, I also recognize that not all aspects of my ancestral religions have supported my growth. I have had to work very hard to discern which faith and which practices I want to keep while releasing what is unhealthy. I know that I don't have to hold onto anything that doesn't support my view of life, my personal values, and how I choose to live—and neither do you.

A fine example is meditation, which was practiced in the yoga community in which I was raised—and later left due to cult-like tendencies. After a lifetime of personal experience and evidence-based outcomes, including 23 years of positive results from recommending meditations to clients for various mental health issues, I feel comfortable continuing the practice. However, I have since let go of the dogma behind the practice; as with my experiences with many religions, so much of it involved guilt and control. After years of wanting to break the patterns of my ancestors, I freed myself from the dysfunctional aspects and focused on its benefits instead.

The role of religion is to offer a safe haven to enjoy the positive aspects of faith. With a strong code of belief in place, we are free to have challenging conversations with ourselves; and no matter what we might uncover, we know that the principles of our religion stand behind us and lend us support.

Organized religion has received some truly bad publicity in the last 50 years or so, resulting in fewer and fewer people participating in some kind of weekly sermon or attending church for prayer and song. With so many religious groups and spiritual communities implicated in controversy—such as rampant abuse—this should come as no surprise. Like a splinter, our instinct is to remove the pain. I understand this desire to walk away, yet I ask you to hold onto the ideology behind your religion. If you find that the ideology works for you, faith is worth saving, even if you discard the organization behind the doctrine.

That said, there is a fine line to walk when it comes to incorporating religion into your life. Like my own spiritual journey, you may have to contemplate how influential a religious creed is in your life, whether it is too much or not enough. Take a look at your belief system and consider whether there may be some dogmatic tendencies within it that are not serving you. For example, the teaching that you are a sinner and must repent in order to be saved. Personally, I don't think that is the message Jesus Christ wanted the world to abide by, but rather to lead by love and kindness—because, deep inside, we are all good.

I stress that this is a very personal journey. There is courage in being with these thoughts, so try not to feel guilt or shame during this introspective process.

WORKSHOP

Try to find some form of faith in your life. You can do this in any way you like; as long as it brings you inner joy and connection, you can find faith anywhere and in anything.

- What speaks to your soul? What brings you joy?

- What leaves you feeling connected with others and/or the earth? Some popular ways to connect include singing, hiking, gardening, creating art, or being involved in a non-denominational community/church.

- How do you find time in your life to have and create experiences that make you feel connected? If you find it difficult to find that time, what can you do to make that time?

- What is something you believe in that is intangible (you are unable to see, hear, or touch it)? Why is it important for you to have this belief?

Finding the Spirit in Spirituality

Faith is essential when pushing through hardships. Faith is optimistic by its very nature and gives us the sense that we can move through anything. We come to believe that, "This, too, shall pass"—that there is always a new day. Faith supports us through pain and suffering because it assures us that we will leave the experience stronger, more knowledgeable and more self-aware. The clients in my office who have a healthy dose of faith (whether spiritual or religious-based) are able to move through disappointment a little easier than those who do not. They trust the process with the certainty that there is always an opportunity to learn and grow. This helps them let go of attachments. They understand that through faith, there is hope.

In the end, having your own faith doctrine is having something that allows you to get out of your own head. Overanalyzing a situation can result in trying to control the situation. Faith, by contrast, involves the sensation of being connected to a greater energy source. It is humbling, which can build healthy self-esteem. It is an inner peace. It is acceptance.

When walking down a path of disappointment—something we will each endure many times in life—faith is an important tool to carry. After all, disappointment and grief can only be processed by going through it. Like a hiker with a backpack full of supplies, you will want to be well-prepared as you travel down this path. Don't forget your own inner compass; it will guide you.

CHAPTER 6

THE TIMELINE TO ACCEPTANCE

WORKING THROUGH THE GRIEF that results from disappointment is a process; I've previously referred to these as stages. This process can be thought of as a timeline, not to be confused with a deadline. There is no minimum or maximum amount of time a person should spend at any given stage. This timeline, which runs from the initial shock of the traumatic experience to eventual acceptance and personal peace, will vary from person to person.

The basics entail:

1. **Shock:** "How could this happen to me?" We feel this stage deep within our body (a somatic response) as we try to make sense of what happened. The mind races or shuts down.

2. **Denial:** "I can't believe this is happening to me." We have trouble accepting the situation as true, simply because we don't want it to be true. Often, we try to pretend like nothing happened. Denial can be a conscious or subconscious reaction. This can last days or even years.

3. **Anger:** "I am furious that this happened. It's not fair!" Anger is a natural part of disappointment. It can move us forward, or it can

cause us to get us stuck. When the latter occurs, it means we are unable to move past the reactive stage of the process.

4. **Wishful Thinking:** "I wish this didn't happen." We fabricate stories to somehow "change" the situation, justifying the event in an attempt to make it okay. By changing the story, it becomes easier to believe that it isn't true or that the pain is fleeting.

5. **Depression:** "I can't move on. The pain is debilitating." We feel stuck in our grief and can no longer see the good in life. The disappointment is replayed over and over in our mind, which further hurts us. This can be a very raw state because we naturally avoid exposing our hurt to others. It can feel isolating. Alternatively, even if we *are* sharing our story with others, they might not be responding in a way that's to our liking, which can make us feel abandoned.

6. **Bargaining:** "If I do XYZ, will the pain go away?" We hope something outside of ourselves will change the event and that we can step past the pain. But there is no way around disappointment—only through it.

7. **Sadness:** "I am so sad this happened. It hurts me to my core." We experience a deep sadness over loss. This is often felt emotionally, but it can manifest itself physically. For some, their view of everything around them is filtered through a lens of sadness. This differs from depression primarily in terms of a person's level of function. A sad person can still handle their day-to-day life, whereas a depressed person will often be unable to do so.

8. **Acceptance:** "What will my life be like once I move past this event, past these thoughts and feelings?" When we start to think of life beyond the pain, its presence is no longer constant. The story of our disappointment starts to change. At this stage, we are

finally growing and evolving. Acceptance of the event means that we have allowed ourselves to see the past with clarity and truly mourn our loss.

9. **Peace:** "I am living my life fully and in the moment." Life becomes more creative. We have learned from the past and are actively moving forward.

Everyone processes life at their own pace, especially in the stages of disappointment. As I mentioned in Chapter 3, we all have our unique qualities (both gifts and shortcomings) which influence how we handle stressful situations and experiences, including pain, trauma, and disappointment. Our uniqueness is a beautiful thing because it gives us the tools to grow as individuals, but it does also mean there is no one-size-fits-all solution to this type of emotional hardship.

THE THREE-MIND APPROACH

Over the years, I have developed a philosophy on why we react to some events differently than others. This cognitive viewpoint, combining my personal experiences with certain yogic concepts, is what I call a **Three-Mind approach** to reactions, comprising of the Negative Mind, the Positive Mind, and the Neutral Mind.

When an event occurs, we always process it first from the stance of the Negative Mind, also known as the Protective Mind. This viewpoint looks at a given situation through the lens of evaluating it for potential danger. We assess whether we need to react immediately, employing various safety precautions or engaging our fight-or-flight response. This lens can become overactive, especially if we have experienced trauma like mental manipulation, physical pain, or emotional confusion. From these prior negative experiences, our Negative Mind becomes less trusting and more aggressive in seeking to protect us.

Our Positive Mind lens—also known as the Projective Mind—is the perspective most impacted by our childhood experiences. It is the part of our mind that sees all possible opportunities. That being said, we don't always *want* to act on all possible outcomes—we still need discernment. An overactive positive mind also means less boundaries. An underdeveloped Positive Mind leads to indecisiveness. If we weren't taught how to think for ourselves, then that means we never learned how to believe in ourselves. Second-guessing becomes second nature. As a result, we have a slower reaction response to situations or rely on others to make choices for us.

(continued next page)

Both the Negative Mind and Positive Mind impact how we view life overall. When they are both functioning in a healthy way, our viewpoint becomes balanced, and we see through our Neutral (or Meditative) Mind. This is the stance of the unattached, curious, Wise-Adult Self. The good news is that we can work on adjusting these lenses through various methods of deep inner growth processing, including self-introspective techniques like journaling and meditation.

My intention when writing this book was initially to guide readers through a more traditional 30-day journey. Yet as I began to put together my thoughts, I kept thinking about my own healing processes. The greatest disappointments in my life were never straightforward and simple. Trying to be at peace with them was a constant back-and-forth movement on the timeline. Some days, I would feel relief, only to slip back into anger or wishful thinking. When we endure disappointment, we do not go up the steps of grief. Because humans are complex creatures, we do not follow strict guidelines. We move in stages applicable to our own stories. It is like riding ocean waves: up and down, over and over, with some swells larger than others. Eventually, you will make it back to the shore.

We can begin the work of healing and growing at any age, as long as we lean into our courage and compassion as we travel through the stages of disappointment. Many years ago, I was working with a woman who had some trauma from her childhood emerge in her 80s. It was painful for her to suddenly remember the abuse she endured in her childhood. She couldn't understand why, after all these years, this memory was coming up. With her trust, I worked with her to open up and talk about this pain. She learned to find moments when she could allow herself to hold open a space for that young girl inside her, but she also learned how to free herself from enduring daily thoughts about the event. Even in her 80s, she didn't want to miss an opportunity to adapt and grow.

As you work through the stages I have laid out in this book, feel free to take some of them on as a challenge. You may need or want to be at any given stage longer than I suggest. You may feel as though you are done with a stage when I am still discussing it. It is normal to jump around on the timeline or feel less-than-okay on certain days. That is perfectly fine. Heal at your own pace, under your own power. My intention is to give you the tools for this journey, but you have to decide when and how to use them yourself.

Learn to trust yourself and be honest with your needs. This book offers an outline, but great artists tend to feel more comfortable improvising. As the artist of your life, paint your own interpretation of disappointment. Have faith in your process and take responsibility for yourself on all levels: body, mind, and soul.

WORKSHOP

How have you processed disappointment in the past? Let's start with some questions:

- How do you relate to or handle disappointment?

- What are the emotions you feel the most when confronting disappointment? Who taught you to feel this emotion? Who acted this way around you when you were growing up?

- Who didn't support or teach you to move through this emotion? Did they also get stuck in this emotion?

- Do you pass through the stages of disappointment quickly, or do you linger? Is there an emotion which is harder for you to be with or handle? What do you do instead of feeling this emotion?

- How did your parental figure(s) deal with or talk about disappointment? When you were hurt as a child (physically or emotionally), how did those around you react to you? Did they coddle you ("oh no, you poor thing") or brush it off ("you are fine")? How do you think this influenced your approach to pain as an adult?

Fear is Natural

Old pain, old trauma, old betrayals... It's all too common for these disappointments to become a part of us. It can even feel like you have a stamp on your forehead: "Hi, my name is _____. I feel like everyone abandons me, so I won't ever really trust you!" You express it in the way you behave around others, in the way you react to stressful situations; it feels like an inherent, unavoidable quality...but you *do* have the power to alter it.

I understand that the prospect of walking through your grief can be terrifying. For example, if one lets go of the belief that they were abandoned in their youth, then who are they now? Do they become someone "new?" What can replace this long-critical part of their personality? It may even be that the injured part of us has helped us thrive: a deep-seated sense of inferiority, for example, might push us to prove ourselves again and again (without ever really enjoying our success, of course). **Grief, once it has put down roots, can establish itself in our very core.** Over time, our selves grow around the grief, defined by it as we are warped by it.

So, what now?

First, know that having compassion and grace for yourself as you approach the healing process is essential. When we are able to understand our own stories (typically created at a time of duress) and experiences (partially formed by those stories) at a profound level, we are able to definitively know what to let go of and what to hold onto. Remember: we don't need to let go of *everything*. Each experience we have endured is a lesson, one whose value does not come from what has happened to us but rather how we sit with it, see it, and respond to it. Keep what you have learned but toss away the pain. You have this ability—you just need the insight and courage to employ it.

For me, the feeling of being abandoned in my youth resulted in me being a very independent person. That is the lesson I kept through my pain. You could put me anywhere in the world, and I could build a life for myself. I make lemonade out of lemons. But I had to work hard to recognize this ability and make this perspective shift happen.

For many years, I was stuck in my storyline of being separated from my parents and sent to a boarding school overseas at the age of eight. People would look at me in shock; and, to be honest, I think a part of me liked that others felt sorry for me. But before long, I would become defensive. I wanted to prove to them that I turned out okay, that my parents were/are good people who did what they thought was right at the time. Some might be horrified over what my parents did, but I have done a lot of work around this adolescent event as an adult. There has been a lot of genuine healing. We have all grown and moved forward. I truly forgive my parents.

Since healing that abandoned inner child, I have softened my view of my story. I have built and maintained a belief within myself that I am complete. I am enough, exactly as I am. With that empowerment, I feel I can trust in the process of life. I can approach other stories—such as my struggle as a teenager to have a connection with my peers—with more wisdom. It is an ongoing journey of healing, and I am always learning from my experiences.

To those of you thinking, "This will never end, and I am so tired of trying," know that this is when life's purpose overlaps with the pain (and even boredom) of healing and growth. It is a contradictory process, at once complicated and simple. The truth is that human beings *need* both purpose and change, even if it can feel tedious. As the Greek philosopher Heraclitus claimed, "The only constant in life is change."

Stage Fright: What Happens When You Feel Stuck

If the disappointment you are working through is fresh, it may be easier to look at because you are still close to it. If you are working on a disappointment from years or even decades ago, however, your life's story has already been impacted by it. These deep roots often mean you may feel stuck as you work on processing the grief. You will be required to really familiarize yourself with each stage and push yourself through the timeline towards acceptance and peace. Depending on your unique makeup, this will be easier for some than others.

For many of us, when we get stuck at a certain stage, we start to get in our heads and feel like a victim as a result. You might ask yourself, "Why am I still here? Why does this keep happening to me?" You might beat yourself up mentally, feeling as though you aren't adequately processing the stages of grief. **Working through the disappointment becomes a disappointment in and of itself.**

Instead of feeling defeated, however, you should use the opportunity to challenge yourself. Challenging yourself, in this context, has everything to do with having the curiosity to contemplate different perspectives. If you believe, "It isn't fair that I have to move on," then the result is you being stuck in anger. Consider the opposite viewpoint instead. What specifically is fair about holding on? What is fair about letting go? Are you losing anything if you *do* let go? Are you gaining anything if you let go? Sometimes stubborn beliefs can hold you hostage to the situation by entrapping you with unforgiving thoughts and feelings. Learn to recognize when you're thinking subjectively, and you may become "unstuck."

I once had to face my own desire for something I did not receive. Although I already had two amazing sons, I wanted to have a daughter. My husband didn't want another child (he felt we were good with two). As he would say, "We can still divide and conquer," which was true. We had a lot going on anyway: two businesses, two children, a household to take care of, and all of our other activities. Still, it was hard for me to shake off that desire. One day, I wondered to myself, *'Will I care about this when I am on my deathbed?'* And I instantly felt an intense feeling sweep through me that said, *'No.'* Right in that moment, I let it go.

Even though I wanted a third child (and especially hoped for the chance we would be blessed with a girl), I was able to hold onto my rational thoughts and emotions. Standing at the threshold of life, I was able to make a clear-headed decision about my fate. I knew that I would not have any regrets if we didn't have a girl. By challenging my beliefs, it set me on a new path. I was free from that old story.

Create room for yourself to ask challenging questions like, "Will I regret this on my deathbed?" After deep introspection, you might be surprised by your own answers. Sometimes beliefs feel so firm and true, but they are often malleable. You can shift your own beliefs and desires by considering opposing views and filtering them through your personal lens. Engage with your authentic self to find the resolution to your issues.

WORKSHOP

When you find yourself stuck with a certain feeling, it could be that you are simply stuck in that story of the stage. Try to deeply analyze your emotions. By getting to know them, you will learn why you carry them around with you. For this exercise, choose a disappointing memory that you constantly revisit.

- What is the most common emotion you feel around this drama/trauma?

- Do others in your life recognize an emotion you've attached to this memory? (For example, "You are so defensive when you talk about this.") If so, what is the emotion?

- What are you afraid of happening if you finally let go of this story and move onto the next stage? What emotion would you need to sit with and understand in order to move on?

- What other fears creep into your head and your heart as you process this event? Are these fears real, or are they made up? Challenge your thinking. Challenge your stance. Challenge these fears.

(continued next page)

We can get stuck in parts of our story—and the emotions associated with it—when we are afraid to look at the experience as a whole. If you cannot face your inner story, you cannot face the fears in your head and in your heart. Until you confront these fears, you will not be able to move through the stages and reach an inner place of peace.

Holding Space for Every Emotion

When processing the dual emotions of anger and pain, there can be a sensation of wanting justice, like you *deserve* some form of recompense. As I mentioned previously, my mother is currently fighting a brain tumor. The sadness and pain I feel worrying about the possible coming loss is big. I can feel its pull within me, reminding me of how I want to spend as much time with her as possible: time of loving connection, of laughter, of just being there for her (and for myself).

But I also must contend with emotions from my past. Before one of my trips to visit her, I packed my bag with items to connect us during my visit: items for spa time, as well as needles and yarn for knitting and crocheting together. I felt waves of pain, anger, and sadness crash within me as I drove to the airport. The adult me wanted to go and spend time with my mom, to cuddle and laugh, to do our nails together, and make pizza. The little girl and teenager inside me wanted to cry and scream because my mother didn't do those things for *me* as a kid, as I was away at boarding school. Both responses are justified; there is no "wrong" way to feel. It is right that I have residual emotions of anger and sadness because my mom wasn't there when I was young. It is also right that the adult me wants to spend as much time with my mom and to make our time together meaningful.

I watched myself as I worked to navigate these opposite emotions. Through deep introspection, I validated that they are all true. I made space for my inner little girl to allow her to feel sad, confused, and lonely. I made the effort to recognize that these are real feelings I felt when I was young and alone at boarding school. I also needed to hold space for my inner teenager, who was still so angry at our parents. She had every right to be mad. Then I held space for the woman I am now, the Wise-Adult Self, who can see all sides of this challenging, multifaceted situation. My Adult Self wanted to create time to be with my mother. In a way, maybe my inner little girl and teenager could also feel the love and connection my mom and I were creating now.

Will our current bonding fix all the pain from the past? The answer is, "No." And that is *okay*. Trying to replace old emotions with new emotions can feel like taking away the pain of the past. Progress comes from holding onto and honoring all those emotions—at the same time. I did it, and I know with practice you can as well.

Although this book is meant to be a self-guiding tool for you to recover from your disappointment, I understand that external help is sometimes required. If you feel you need additional support, I recommend you work with a licensed psychotherapist. There is courage in asking for help, and I applaud you for even considering it.

CHAPTER 7

STAGES OF HEALING

A S YOU GO THROUGH life, you *will* encounter disappointments. Whether this is fortunate or unfortunate comes down to your ability (and, more importantly, willingness) to turn these events into learning experiences. That is what we each must strive to accomplish. There's no way to live a life without disappointment, after all—there's no place on Earth without its share of dramas and traumas. Our objective is to handle these various disappointments and to learn from them.

Preparing for Processing

Before you start this healing journey, it is important to take inventory. What are you carrying around with you? What past events—your relationships, traumatic experiences, negative criticism—are still influencing you to this day? To recognize these disappointments is to acknowledge them, which is the first step in recovering from the pain they've left behind. It is about making sense of the event by giving it a new meaning, which cannot happen until you understand its current meaning.

I would like you to take some time to think and feel through your past pain and trauma. Make note of which events or situations you revisit the most, whether you quietly replay them in your mind or tell others about them. If you haven't already done so for previous workshop prompts, start compiling a list of disappointments in your life which still impact you today. You don't need to go into full detail of each event: a title, an associated word, or writing the name of a person involved is enough to categorize the experience for now. If you've already curated a list, it is time to revisit them.

All of these disappointments set before you, especially the largest and most painful ones, combine to create the lens through which you view and approach life. It influences how you work, how you speak to loved ones, and how you behave around new people. It is time to bring this trauma out from within you and take stock of it. If you ignore it, you can't change it. Remember what I said earlier: if you can't self-reflect, you won't self-correct.

As you work on this list, think about things that you have brought up multiple times with family members, partners, friends, or a therapist. For me, because I often felt embittered towards my parents, it was, "Hey, mom. Remember when you sent me off to boarding school and I felt abandoned?" It can be embarrassing to admit to some of these feelings, but it is important to remain open and honest with yourself. Resentment usually involves emotions that need resolution.

Or maybe there is something about yourself that a loved one continually brings up; write that down, too. By confronting those remarks, you can see what role you play in their criticism. Maybe you are exacerbating the issue because of some thought or sentiment you are carrying around, something called **unconscious trauma.** Even if we can't see it, we may still be reacting in a way that is hurting another person who was part of the narrative. This is not a malicious act, but rather one that has been quietly written into part of our story.

Go back even further. Reflect on your younger years: elementary school, middle school, high school, college. Spend time in the mind of your young adult self, entering the workforce for the first time. In psychotherapy, clients routinely talk about events from the past, events that somehow left an imprint on them which affects their present life, often because of residual pain. We can sometimes attach ourselves to this trauma, keeping us in certain thinking patterns. With work, we can unleash ourselves from these patterns and view life through a clearer lens.

WORKSHOP

By reading up to this point, you have already contemplated the past disappointments of your life. Maybe you have set this book down and thought to yourself, "Why *do* I allow this past narrative of drama and trauma to continually impact how I live, how I treat others, and how I view myself? How can this change?"

Now it is time to take those disappointments and make a commitment to alter your story. Retrieve your list of disappointments from previous workshops and note which you want to focus on. You don't need to do all of them all at once. Take a moment—maybe even a day—and let them sit there on the paper. It takes courage to acknowledge that you need help working on these specific events. You are saying, "I want to make a change in my life. I am *ready* for this change." When you're mentally prepared, answer these questions as best you can.

- What story from the past do you repeat the most (whether in conversations with others or mentally to yourself)? Why do you think you keep returning to it?

- What emotion do you feel most often in relation to this event? What are some past events which left you feeling that emotion the strongest? How did you interpret this event or this emotion at the time?

- What events in your past impact how you feel about yourself now? What is this feeling? Inadequate, alone, angry, sad?

- What are you most afraid of? Does anyone in your family share this same fear? Write about how you learned to be afraid of this.

Putting in the Work

In the following pages, you will find a 30-step guide to walk you through the stages of disappointment. This is meant to serve as a map for you to follow, but remember that everyone is different. For some, the process of moving through a past (or current) disappointment may take 30 days or more, while others might find that they can move faster and take fewer than 30 days. There is no right or wrong way to arrive at your destination, as long as you get there. Don't fault yourself if you take longer. The intention is to grieve and move forward, but this can only be achieved by moving through the disappointments and letdowns in life. If we are unable to do this, we can get stuck in any or all of the different emotions of grief. Take your time—as long as you are taking that time to work on yourself.

While it is important to be kind to yourself throughout, it is also important to continually push yourself; otherwise you can get stuck in one stage/emotion for a long time. Again, the timeline of your healing process may vary, but there should always be some movement—even if it is back and forth. This offers you chances to learn about yourself, how you think and hold on to ideas and feelings. If you find that you tend to get stuck in the "why is this happening to me" stage or the "it doesn't bother me" stage, work with that knowledge. Contemplate why that is so.

Some people get stuck in the depression or anger stage for 40 years. Is this serving them? No, of course not. But they have a difficult time letting go of a story that has embedded itself into their personality and viewpoint. They may believe that coming to peace with the situation translates to them being okay with it. That is not always true. **Forgiveness is about setting yourself free from the pain but holding onto its lessons, which is the goal of moving through these stages.**

Forgiving the event doesn't mean forgetting it. For me, I could hold onto the story that I was abandoned and that my parents didn't care about me, *or* I could view it as my parents being lost at that stage of their life and believing they were doing the right thing by sending me to a boarding school. Either way, the lesson I carry from that trauma is that I am a strong and resilient individual for living through it. I turned the pain from my own experience into unconditional love and loyalty to my children. This healing process took years of grit and perseverance to find and accept my inner strength. Aim to cultivate this same power: the ability to detach yourself from the harmful elements of your past while retaining the positive lessons.

You may also find that a private journey, just being with yourself during these 30 stages, may be exactly what you need. This will allow you to sit within the stage you are in and learn about yourself. On a daily basis, you will be required to be silent and listen to your thoughts. Try to meditate on these thoughts while on a walk or in a quiet space, then journal your feelings. Ask yourself to look at each stage with a different perspective, depending on the tools and insights provided. By doing so, you can challenge your own thoughts and clear a path towards a peaceful resolution or a reframing of the event. You can open yourself to awareness and growth. You can create your own liberation.

Not everyone can benefit from a private journey, however. If you find you need extra guidance, **I highly recommend working with a licensed mental health worker such as a psychotherapist.** Because internalized grief is big, deep, and often childhood-related, it helps to have someone who knows how to navigate around trauma and is trained to hold that space for you. They will be able to support you as you look at difficult thoughts and emotions surrounding your disappointment. We can often be so stuck in our own view of the event; we can't see it any other way. A therapist can help you shift this perspective. (Please note: when first working with someone, you may need some time to build a safe and healthy environment with your therapist. Take the time to build this trust relationship so that you can explore deep emotions together.)

Seeking outside help does *not* mean that you are weak. Unfortunately, this is an attitude that is held by many and prevents those in pain from reaching out. **Seeking help means that you are cognizant enough to recognize that you could benefit from that extra support.** It is a reaffirmation of your commitment to address this problem, this disappointment—to learn and grow and shift and heal from it so that you can finally let go of it and move onwards in your life. Even though I am a licensed psychotherapist, I have personally asked for support, both with a therapist and within group therapy. This greatly helped me during my own healing journey.

Perhaps you don't relate to either extreme end of the spectrum. Perhaps you don't want to go on a private journey, but you also don't want to detail your innermost thoughts with a mental health professional. That's perfectly fine; you can toe the line in the middle by reaching out to friends or family members that you trust. Don't be shy about asking someone else to join you on this journey. Perhaps they have some grief to work through, too. This can actually prove to be a bonding experience, helping to build or strengthen a relationship on a whole new level.

If you want additional support that doesn't involve another individual, consider taking up some sort of somatic activity. Some may opt for a "smash room" (a controlled environment in which patrons destroy designated objects), while others may prefer pushing themselves physically (running a marathon, bike riding, or lifting weights). These activities can often help us let go of pent-up thoughts and feelings because they encourage release. You can practice them with an intention towards letting go of certain emotions, like anger, frustration, and even sadness. Somatic activities can teach us that it is okay to let go, providing an inner transformation through outer expression. I have tried this method myself, and I can confirm it has worked.

When you choose to start your journey, you may decide to start with a "minor" disappointment (something small and fleeting) and, upon successfully overcoming it, move on to address a "major" disappointment (often deep-rooted and derived from childhood trauma). Perhaps you feel the opposite and would prefer tackling the biggest issue first, clearing the path to handle smaller complaints. Only you can determine where a disappointment falls on your priority list. Feel free to return to this book and the 30 stages as you work through each of your disappointments.

However you choose to approach the process, I hope that the tools in this book give you the space, courage, and grace to ask yourself what you need. All I request is that you make a commitment to stay on this journey until you reach a state of mind in which you feel freer from this drama and/or trauma.

Let's get started…

▬ STAGE 1 ▬
SHOCK & DENIAL

IMPULSIVE REACTION

A Knee-Jerk View of the Situation

"What! What the...? What the ****!?"

EMOTIONAL REACTION

The Story (Real or Imagined) You are Telling Yourself

You just found out the bad news. You did not see it coming and cannot believe the outcome, or perhaps you saw it coming but prayed it wouldn't happen. This is the "can't be true" stage. The situation could involve a relationship ending, a sudden and tragic death, losing a job, or any other life-shifting event. No matter what happened, it feels like you've just been hit by a truck. You are in total shock as you process this sudden disruption in your life.

PHYSICAL REACTION

What is Happening in Your Body

Your adrenaline is rushing. You feel tension in your stomach, shoulders, and chest. It can be hard to complete tasks due to the anxiety, even something as simple as eating or maintaining basic hygiene (bathing and/or brushing teeth). Chronic stress can make it difficult to focus; nothing feels real. Some individuals suffer from digestive issues, resulting in vomiting and/or diarrhea.

PSYCHOLOGICAL REACTION

What is Happening in Your Brain

When we are in shock, we forget our connection with the world. You may feel alone, even when people are around you. It is normal to feel anxious and confused. Many, when in shock, forget how to breathe properly and consequently hyperventilate. You may begin to associate breathing with something painful or scary, increasing your emotional stress. Poor breath support can reinforce negative processing cycles, causing you to get stuck in a loop of believing all of your anxiety-induced thoughts, no matter their validity. When we breathe consciously, we *feel* more; this self-awareness helps to ground us, stifling reactive thoughts and actions.

CHANGING THE STORY

SPIRITUAL COGNITION

A Mindful View of the Situation

Shocking events can cause us to lose control of ourselves. Sometimes this can result in hyperventilation, further increasing emotional stress. Remember to breathe as you pass through this stage, relying on deep belly breaths. Inhale through the nose, and exhale through the mouth. Count to 10. Splash cold water on your face. Try to avoid driving. Drink plenty of water. Don't forget to eat but be careful not to overindulge.

MENTAL FOCUS

A New Perspective to Reset Your Thoughts

"I am on a journey, and the road isn't always smooth or straightforward."

QUESTIONS TO PONDER AND JOURNAL

What just happened in your life? First, write down the facts. Work on connecting to what is actually happening rather than how your mind is trying to make sense of it. If this is an old memory, write about the facts from that time. If this is a new disappointment in your life, writing down the facts will help stabilize you while you reel from the initial shock and resulting emotions (like pain and confusion).

Whether your pain stems from an old event (such as childhood trauma) or a new event (such as ending a relationship), focusing on the facts—not the feelings—will help ground you as you work on processing complex emotions related to this disappointment, like shock, confusion, pain, anger, and guilt.

TOOLS TO GUIDE YOU

Get grounded as soon as possible. Even though the pain is deep, remember that the pain itself cannot kill you. Start with daily walks, taking the same route each time to create a new pattern of familiarity. There is a dramatic change happening in your life, so having a routine to depend on will help you. Listen to your favorite music on these walks, or even try listening to meditation chanting for focus.

Don't hesitate to reach out to someone for help. Many of us who have experienced trauma (especially childhood trauma) will pack its fallout away into a box deep within our minds. Sometimes we keep that box hidden for decades, just to avoid seeing it and reliving the pain.

Remember that you are alive. Try to maintain healthy habits to remind yourself of your presence on Earth and all the potential inherent in life. Again, even though it hurts so much, the pain itself cannot kill you. Tell yourself, "I am present. I will treat my emotional wounds like a physical wound: with patience and conscious care."

STAGE 2
SHOCK

IMPULSIVE REACTION
A Knee-Jerk View of the Situation

"I can't believe this really happened!"

EMOTIONAL REACTION
The Story (Real or Imagined) You are Telling Yourself

You may have unwarranted absolutist thoughts, such as, "They were always thinking of leaving me and were leading me on this entire time. I am so stupid that I didn't see this coming. All men/women/people are assholes who will hurt me like this. I can't trust anyone. What can I change to stop this from happening again?"

PHYSICAL REACTION
What is Happening in Your Body

The fight-or-flight response is activated due to your adrenals pumping, which can cause volatile physical reactions on wildly different spectrums. This may not necessarily involve running away or combating the event; you may even want to try to freeze or fix the situation. The response will be different for each person. It can feel like a weak or rapid pulse. There are small glimpses of fear and anger in your peripheral, but mostly you are still in shock. Your chest hurts. You may be having digestive problems, particularly constipation. You are crying uncontrollably. You are forgetful. You want to be alone a lot.

PSYCHOLOGICAL REACTION
What is Happening in Your Brain

As the shock washes over you, you are forced to confront the harsh reality of the situation. It is difficult to process the steps that brought you to this point; in this vulnerable state, you may feel shame and even blame yourself for what has happened. You may start to consider that you have been in denial over events leading up to this situation, which in itself can be quite shocking.

During this time, you may want to avoid being around others and feel the need to hide. You may isolate yourself in the process. If this disappointment stems from a past betrayal, then you may start evaluating your having been in denial of this pain for so long. You ask yourself, "How have I just been living my life? How have I managed?" That is the key: you *have* managed, and you *are* still here. You can still be whole, even though you currently feel broken. A damaged pot can be repaired as long as you have the pieces, patience, and willpower to put it back together. When we are in shock, we can't always see this.

CHANGING THE STORY

SPIRITUAL COGNITION

A Mindful View of the Situation

Be aware of yourself. Remember that you are still in a relationship with yourself. This journey through the grieving process will require you to be consciously aware and introspective. Take a look in the mirror. Look at your eyes. Look into your eyes. See yourself. You are *here.*

This period of time of shock (and denial) is all about getting back into your body/mind and remaining present in your life. This sometimes hurts, but you will be okay. Take it one step at a time. Even though it is painful, remind yourself that you are on a journey of healing—and every journey takes time.

MENTAL FOCUS

A New Perspective to Reset Your Thoughts

"I am present. I am alive."

QUESTIONS TO PONDER AND JOURNAL

Write about what shocks you the most about your current situation. Is there something about it that is not shocking? Are there aspects of your life before this event that you now view differently? How did you manage difficult moments relating to this person/experience in the past? How can you apply your previous coping mechanisms to your current situation?

TOOLS TO GUIDE YOU

Physical movements can help connect us to our emotions because we feel them throughout our entire body rather than just in our minds. It asks us to be self-aware. This helps prevent our thoughts from becoming stagnant which aids us in our journey. Look into joining a yoga class or boxing class. Dancing is another amazing tool to get you back into your body and to keep the energy flowing. I mean it: put this book down, go to Spotify or Apple Music and pick the dance generation you love (I recommend an 80s or 90s playlist) and move for at least three minutes. That's the average length of a single pop song, so you may find you want to continue even after the song ends. Get moving and stay moving.

Hydrotherapy is another great form of physical therapy, as it supports our nervous system by getting our blood flowing. In many cultures, water is seen as a source of transformation and a symbol of healing, of letting go. The best way to practice hydrotherapy is to rub a natural oil all over your body before starting a shower. Turn the water in your shower to cold. Start by getting only your limbs wet, rubbing the cold water over your hands, arms, feet, and legs. Next, step your whole body into the shower and continue rubbing the water over yourself. Make sure the cold water reaches your entire body. Laugh, sing, cry—express yourself in whatever way feels necessary and good. You only need to do this for two to three minutes. Once you are finished, you can soak under warm water or get out and put on some comfortable clothing. Either way, try to relax.

▬▬▬ STAGE 3 ▬▬▬
DENIAL & ISOLATION

IMPULSIVE REACTION

A Knee-Jerk View of the Situation

"This can't be happening. No one can know what I am going through."

EMOTIONAL REACTION

The Story (Real or Imagined) You are Telling Yourself

The pain is overwhelming. It is felt both physically and emotionally; you cannot stop thinking about what happened. At this stage, we often feel as though no one will understand us, further isolating us in our own pain. It can be shameful to relive the situation—including the events that led up to it—causing us to hide from others.

Isolation is an emotional tool we utilize as a reaction. By isolating ourselves, we isolate the pain within ourselves so as not to feel it so strongly. It is a coping mechanism. In the short-term, it can be acceptable; however, in the long-term, it numbs us to our emotions. When feelings get suppressed within our bodies, we turn to bad habits.

PHYSICAL REACTION

What is Happening in Your Body

You are losing weight or gaining weight because you are not eating or are eating all the time. Your sleep has been impacted; you toss and turn all night, or you sleep all day. Your chest hurts. You are holding everything in, so you start feeling constipated. Now your body feels bloated. You may find yourself crying uncontrollably. Because it is difficult to concentrate, you are often forgetful. You prefer being physically alone.

PSYCHOLOGICAL REACTION
What is Happening in Your Brain

Denial is the refusal of accepting something as true. In a cruel paradox, not being honest with yourself feels like you are somehow protecting yourself. Sometimes it's because it feels too shocking to be real, but other times it can simply be because we hope it's fake. This is one way we try to protect ourselves from the pain of the truth. But denial is like the water which boils the frog: if you continue to ignore your situation, it will only hurt you in the end.

As you deny the situation, you become more rigid and stuck. You think this deep pain can't be true. You are not being honest with yourself, which can cause more pain and keep you stuck in a stage of denial.

When I was a little girl, I was sent to live with another family in America while my parents remained in Germany. I lived that entire first year in denial. I kept thinking, "This can't be true. I will wake up soon and be in my bed. In Germany. In my parents' home..." I wished to reverse the pain by living in my own reality. However, we need to confront and deal with the reality of our situation in order to move on from the pain associated with it. There is no way around it, only through it.

CHANGING THE STORY

SPIRITUAL COGNITION
A Mindful View of the Situation

Isolation can feel like a deep disconnection from everything—and I do mean everything. Despite billions of people on Earth and the possibility to instantly connect with others via social media, we can still feel alone in this world. This is when having a connection to a higher power (whatever that means to you) can be helpful.

Your belief in a higher source does not necessarily have to be religiously based or dogmatic in any way—so long as it is a spiritual practice rooted in faith. It is not about right or wrong, good or bad. It is about the energy which flows from the earth, into our bodies, and back to the earth. Maybe it is time to lean on a source that you can't hear, see, or touch. What do you have faith in?

MENTAL FOCUS

A New Perspective to Reset Your Thoughts

"I know I am connected to a source greater than myself when I feel the sun on my face and the wind through my hair."

QUESTIONS TO PONDER AND JOURNAL

Do you view denial and/or isolation as a form of protection? If so, how has this served you? Was this a learned behavior from your childhood? If so, who taught you this avoidance tactic? Have you learned anything from being in denial and/or in isolation, or has the situation worsened?

Remember: this mentality can only sustain itself for so long before it becomes damaging. You need to be present with yourself so you can ask yourself what you need. Only *you* can initiate the healing that you require.

TOOLS TO GUIDE YOU

If you feel you are not in your body, take a cold shower daily (two to three minutes) until you feel aligned with yourself again. Shock yourself back into your body. Wake up! Studies have found that hydrotherapy strengthens our nervous system, which supports us when maneuvering through emotional drama and trauma. When our nervous systems are strong, we can process what is happening around us with awareness rather than with a fight, flight, freeze, or fix response.

If you are grieving from an old trauma, try getting in touch with your younger identity. Locate pictures of yourself from a time that directly led to this event. Look at these photos. It may be difficult at first, but you need to be able to separate who you are now from who you were back then. Keep these photos around, as you will need to return to them throughout your healing journey.

■ STAGE 4 ■
DENIAL & ISOLATION

IMPULSIVE REACTION

A Knee-Jerk View of the Situation

"Is this a dream? I wish this would end. I feel so alone."

EMOTIONAL REACTION

The Story (Real or Imagined) You are Telling Yourself

You are trying to figure out the story you are telling yourself through this pain, but it is hard to be fully honest with yourself. You are still holding onto the idea of the person or thing you have lost. Everything seems bleak compared to the "before." During this time of disappointment, we can stew in feelings of jealousy. We compare ourselves with others, further isolating ourselves.

You are trying to make sense of the event. You are playing it over in your mind, viewing it through different lenses. You just don't want it to be true. What is the story you are telling yourself with this disappointment? With this pain? With this betrayal? Are you sharing these stories with others in hopes that they will validate your beliefs (whether or not they are true)?

Once your story starts to change and becomes more reflective of reality, you can begin to feel less alone. This process may feel so uncomfortable that you want to stay in denial. It is scary to be confronted with the truth—and even scarier to accept it. For some, it may be that you haven't told anyone, and the thought of sharing your story makes it feel too real. You still don't want it to be true. However, acknowledging the reality will carry you out of your denial.

PHYSICAL REACTION

What is Happening in Your Body

You may still be feeling discomfort in your upper stomach. Digestive issues may persist, whether diarrhea or constipation. When we go through emotional drama and/or trauma, it weakens our immune system. This is the time to focus on getting good sleep and maintaining nutritionally balanced eating habits (plus potential supplements as recommended by a licensed nutritionist). You may also feel pangs of pain as you are reminded of what has happened. You want to run away from your emotions in an attempt to mask the physical discomfort, but this will only delay your healing process. Try to remain in the now; this will also aid in better sleep, as you are not ruminating through intrusive thoughts (which often leads to anxiety).

PSYCHOLOGICAL REACTION

What is Happening in Your Brain

The mind thinks in polarities, which is why your mind wants to make sense of things as right or wrong, good or bad. During this stage, we may fabricate a story—itself another form of denial—in order to ratio-nalize the situation. This is a dangerous stage because many of us can get stuck here; it can feel good to ignore everything and focus on our own preferred truth. We start to believe the stories we've made up to make sense of the painful event.

For some of us, feelings of shock, pain, and/or anger can result in even more complicated mental states such as despair or depression. Wanting to escape these feelings of despair can cause some to feel a need to "disappear," which can manifest as suicidal ideations. If you feel this way, please know that you are not alone. Help is out there. There are people who can and want to support you during this healing journey. You are important—your presence on Earth is important—and suicide is not the path to freedom.

If you are located in the United States and looking to speak with a counselor, reach out to the national hotline by calling or texting

988; help is available 24 hours for English and Spanish speakers. You can also dial 911 for help. Because every country will offer different services, you may want to research what your local options are when seeking additional assistance if you are outside of the United States.

CHANGING THE STORY

SPIRITUAL COGNITION
A Mindful View of the Situation

Allow certain questions to be seeds about your potential future. For example, "Do I want this situation to be the end of my life or the beginning of a new life?" Your life will not stop here if you learn the lesson that is in this experience; you can take it as an opportunity to grow and prosper. Here is the thing: bad things happen to everyone. The good news is that, with awareness and focus, we all can move through the bad things and evolve. I have seen it happen again and again.

MENTAL FOCUS
A New Perspective to Reset Your Thoughts

"I am in control of my own life story."

QUESTIONS TO PONDER AND JOURNAL

If you can, write with pen and paper, not on a computer. Studies show that writing supports the healing process because it brings internal focus and clarity, helping us to grieve and increasing happiness in the long run. Try writing in a stream of consciousness style, letting your thoughts flow straight onto the page. What are the emotions linked to this hurt, this situation, this past trauma? Is there a theme in your life regarding this event? How is this making you feel right now? What part of the story is hurting the most? Why?

If you can, write with pen and paper, not on a computer. Studies show that writing supports the healing process because it brings internal focus and clarity, helping us to grieve and increasing happiness in the long run. Try writing in a stream of consciousness style, letting your thoughts flow straight onto the page.

TOOLS TO GUIDE YOU

If you are stuck on a specific emotion, listen to TED Talks, short-form podcasts, and/or short audiobooks with a focus on that emotion to help you understand and process it. Sit outside or enjoy a walk while you listen. Allow the growth experience from others to support you on your journey.

If you are open to meditation, try meditating in 4/1 segmented breathing. This is a simple and easy breathing meditation to support the racing mind; it helps placate your emotions, calming you down internally.

4/1 Segmented Breathing

- Sit or lie down in a comfortable space. Try to keep your back straight, as this impacts your breathing. You want open and unobstructed airflow.

- Close your eyes. Close your mouth. Hold your hands loosely in your lap (if you are sitting) or over your belly (if you are lying down).

- Inhale through the nose in four segments (four little sniffs in), and then exhale through the nose in one segment (one slow breath out). You can count your breaths on your own, or you can listen to meditation music for guidance.

STAGE 5
DENIAL & ISOLATION
(ANGER & VICTIMHOOD)

IMPULSIVE REACTION

A Knee-Jerk View of the Situation

"It is everyone else's fault. No one understands me. Why am I so alone? I feel a little crazy. Okay, I feel 'a lot' crazy..."

EMOTIONAL REACTION

The Story (Real or Imagined) You are Telling Yourself

Even if you are in isolation from others, you are still having conversations with yourself. The stories you tell yourself during this time will serve as the outline for stories you will tell yourself in the future. It is important to be honest with yourself as you process the events that have unfolded—but be kind to yourself. This is the first step in removing yourself from denial and moving forward in life.

Our desire is to hold onto the situation in some capacity: the lover, the friend, the job, the community, the religion. It can feel like grasping at straws. During this time of facing what has happened, we feel isolated and alone. We can't really see all the sides because we are too close to the situation and the emotions it has stirred up. We get locked into feelings of jealousy, comparing ourselves with others ("poor me") which makes us feel even more alone.

PHYSICAL REACTION

What is Happening in Your Body

You may have noticed frequent urination or even had issues with a urinary infection. Eastern philosophy believes that we hold fear in our kidneys; during times when we are in shock and/or a denial stage for too long or too deeply, this negative energy can sink into our kidneys and bladder. Studies have shown that while the body is under stress, our bladder muscles unconsciously squeeze, making it harder to relax. Physical stress can also increase your blood pressure, which impacts your memory and the ability to problem-solve. This is why we often make poor choices when in emotional distress, like reaching out to an ex-partner. Don't beat yourself up if you make a mistake during this healing process. Your emotions directly influence your rational thinking skills, thanks to that high blood pressure. That is why it is important to try to relax.

PSYCHOLOGICAL REACTION

What is Happening in Your Brain

From my experience as a psychotherapist, I have noticed that most people go through some kind of dramatic and/or traumatic life shakeup every three or seven years—voluntarily or otherwise. Humans are not structured to live the same process *ad nauseam*. If we don't actively create change, something outside of us will.

Use this opportunity to learn and grow. Many of us enjoy being in the comfort of denial and isolation rather than committing to self-reflection, but that's not helpful. Sitting with your emotions can actually help you through the stages of disappointment. Let go of your beliefs and the expectations you've set upon yourself. Shake out your body and free your mind.

When the walls of denial and shock start to shift, we feel a rawness, a vulnerability. We feel exposed; sometimes we can even feel like an idiot. Anger is the next step as we enter into a reaction stage, which is all about protecting yourself. This often occurs when we finally admit that the event *did* happen, it *does* hurt, and that we *are* afraid of the outcome. It is not uncommon to jump from denial to sadness or depression, and anger is very close behind.

CHANGING THE STORY

SPIRITUAL COGNITION
A Mindful View of the Situation

In order to rid yourself of stagnant energy, try doing Body Drops. Eastern philosophy believes that this practice shakes out our internal blueprint, allowing us to be cognizant of the life changes we must make. Body Drops encourage *chakra* energy to flow so we are less likely to feel stuck. Jostle your mind and body out of shock so that you can better process the situation. See the Tools to Guide You in this section for an explanation of how to practice Body Drops.

If you're uncomfortable with an Eastern approach, a Western intervention might employ a different form of physical exercise, such as cardio (like shaking and dancing) or even visiting a smash room. In *Waking the Tiger: Healing Trauma*, Peter Levine talks about this kind of healing through body shifting—how human beings instinctively react to stress differently than other mammals. There is a research study about polar bears who, after being shot with a tranquilizer gun and immobilized, would shake violently for a period of time after waking up. Once the shaking was done, the bear would run off like nothing happened. Animals still have this innate response to "shake it off," while humans often don't know how to naturally release stress. We need to do the physical work just as much as the mental work.

Many people go for a run or hit the gym when they are upset. It's all about getting your heart rate up and channeling an elevated emotional state into an active, productive physical state. There are more and more psychotherapists who are trained in somatic experiencing with a focus on relieving stress from the physical body where trauma and drama is stored. If you need extra support in this field, look for therapists trained in Internal Family Systems (IFS), eye movement desensitization and reprocessing (EMDR), somatic experiencing (SE), and/or some yoga.

American psychiatrist Dr. David Burns, author of *Feeling Good: The New Mood Therapy*, once had a client suffer a panic attack in his office. She couldn't breathe and was sure she was actually having a heart attack. She kept repeating how she felt out of control. Dr. Burns had her stand up and start running in place, right there in his office. She told him, "I can't. I can't breathe." He said to keep running. After a few minutes, she actually started breathing more deeply. She had released her negative thought patterns and given the space to breathe normally. Her mood changed, right then and there.

When we are stuck in an emotion from our drama and/or trauma, our thoughts can take over—no matter how rational or irrational they are. When we're already in a state of duress, fear will lead the way. Being physically active shifts our mental focus, and then we can work on changing our emotional focus.

MENTAL FOCUS

A New Perspective to Reset Your Thoughts

"I can sit with hard feelings. I know they won't kill me."

QUESTIONS TO PONDER AND JOURNAL

Confronting reality is difficult because it means sitting with the truth. It may be painful to face these questions and to have an honest conversation with yourself, but it is only a passing stage on this journey of healing.

Who are you? What do you live by? What emotion are you suppressing? What emotion are you feeling the most? How does this reflect on the situation you are dealing with?

Confronting reality is difficult because it means sitting with the truth. It may be painful to face these questions and to have an honest conversation with yourself, but it is only a passing stage on this journey of healing.

TOOLS TO GUIDE YOU

If you find yourself stuck in denial and shock, that means it is time to shake things up internally. When we have trouble changing, it may be because we are physically stuck within our body—not just our minds.

This can happen especially with those who have encountered sexual and/or physical abuse. We must shake up our bodies from within.

Some ways to shake up the body include:

• **Practice Body Drops.** Sit on the floor with your legs crossed or stretched out. Place your hands on the floor, at your thighs. Use your hands to lift your body up, then drop it back down onto the floor. You have control over how fast or high you go.

• **Dance like no one is watching.** Dance hard and fast, like you are in a mosh pit at a Metallica concert. Stomp around. Yell. Wave your arms up and down. Move your whole body.

• **Rock and roll on the ground.** Find some space on a soft floor and roll around. This all-over massage helps move the energy in your body.

STAGE 6
ANGER

IMPULSIVE REACTION
A Knee-Jerk View of the Situation

"What the ****! I'm so pissed this happened. I am seeing red... I need everyone to know what happened to me, or I might become destructive!"

EMOTIONAL REACTION
The Story (Real or Imagined) You are Telling Yourself

Do you feel the need to tell everyone how angry and unfair this all is? Have you told someone all about the frustration you feel? At this stage, you may want nothing more than an audience to hear your story, to validate what you're feeling. For better or worse, social media can often fill this need, especially if the disappointment was within an organization or community.

You may notice you have a short fuse. You are easy to irritate—anything or anyone can be the culprit. You are quick to snap at people. Emotional boundaries you once held up have deteriorated, and you now find it difficult to feel anything but anger (and sometimes sadness, which is often masked by anger).

PHYSICAL REACTION
What is Happening in Your Body

While fear is stored in our kidneys and bladder, anger is held in our liver. Think about someone who has had too much to drink and becomes belligerent under the influence. Alcohol affects the liver which causes us to lash out. If you are already prone to angry outbursts, abstain from alcohol as you process your grief in this stage.

PSYCHOLOGICAL REACTION
What is Happening in Your Brain

Anger is a form of protection that our nervous system implements to deal with the overwhelming information it is processing. You may be experiencing residual denial, which results in open attacks against anyone who is trying to confront you with the truth. During this time, try to accept different perspectives without bias. With betrayal and anger, we sometimes start to distrust everyone around us. Realize that others *do* want to help you. People who care for you tend to have your best interests at heart.

Note that anger isn't always an inappropriate response; what's important is learning how to experience it in a healthy way. If we are unable to harness our anger, we can get stuck in this stage and hurt those around us, physically and/or emotionally. Anger is one of the first reactions because we often don't know how to be sad and vulnerable. This can be especially difficult for men, as many are discouraged from being emotional and vulnerable from a young age. There is a fear that power will be lost by being too open. This is learned behavior passed down from generation to generation, often from father figures holding up a veil of strength. However, it is only a veil; we are *all* susceptible to *all* emotions. Doing the work now will help you break negative patterns for future generations.

CHANGING THE STORY

SPIRITUAL COGNITION
A Mindful View of the Situation

When you sit with your anger, do you feel your current age or younger? Residual hurt can be sourced from different times in your life. The introspection required during yoga and meditation can excavate hidden emotions, allowing us to look at them and process them fully. Anger in particular can cause us to be very reactive. Like a kid trying to drive a truck, eventually we will lose control and crash. Mindful practices like yoga and meditation can support us while self-reflecting during the stages of anger, allowing us to be more aware and responsive in our lives. It allows us to put a foot on the brake, slowing us down.

MENTAL FOCUS

A New Perspective to Reset Your Thoughts

"Being angry is not bad; it is how we express our anger."

QUESTIONS TO PONDER AND JOURNAL

As we come into our anger, we are not yet ready to see the silver lining. Do not force a lesson onto yourself during this time. This time is all about getting to know your anger. It is not inherently wrong to be mad; it is all about how we act when this emotion is guiding us.

How do you express your anger? What feeds your anger? Who in your childhood was angry like this? Who didn't stop you from behaving this way as a child?

As we come into our anger, we are not yet ready to see the silver lining. Do not force a lesson onto yourself during this stage. This time is all about getting to know your anger. It is not inherently wrong to be mad; it is all about how we act when this emotion is guiding us.

TOOLS TO GUIDE YOU

Try meditation to face your anger. Sit on the floor or in a chair, keeping your spine straight. Stretch your arms out from your shoulders, holding them parallel to the floor, with one hand facing up and the other facing down. Close your eyes. Begin to breathe long and deep. Your inhales should be a hiss-like breath into the mouth. Then, slowly exhale through the nose. Continue for 6–11 minutes.

When you inhale through the hissing mouth, you may find yourself making really expressive faces. Let yourself feel your anger. For some, this will be easy—maybe even too easy. For others, this will feel uncomfortable. The point of this exercise is for you to be conscious and aware during the experience, so it is normal to feel slightly uncomfortable.

If it helps support you, you can use this meditation with the free music included with this book.

Sun Salutation is a practice that exists in various branches of yoga, including Hatha, Kundalini, and Vinyasa. This yoga sequence uses our breath to open our body, allowing for movement both physically and spiritually. What I like about this flow sequence is that you can do it anywhere, anytime you need energetic support. Start practicing three cycles every morning or right before bed. You can find a diagram and instructions for this practice on my website.

STAGE 7
ANGER

IMPULSIVE REACTION
A Knee-Jerk View of the Situation

"Why would they do this to me? Who the hell do they think they are? I am afraid to be angry. I may lose control."

EMOTIONAL REACTION
The Story (Real or Imagined) You are Telling Yourself

We sometimes express anger in order to cover up the true emotion we are experiencing, especially deep sadness and sorrow. For some of us, feeling sad feels like a weakness—and it is a scary state in which to get stuck. It means we feel vulnerable, which in turn means we feel susceptible to more pain. You may notice yourself starting to isolate away from others again because it feels safer to be alone. You might think, "No one gets me anyway."

PHYSICAL REACTION
What is Happening in Your Body

You may have trouble sleeping. The anger feels like an electric current in your body, constantly buzzing. It is distracting as it vibrates through every cell of your body. You can't sleep because of these ongoing racing thoughts.

PSYCHOLOGICAL REACTION
What is Happening in Your Brain

By denying the situation, we deny ourselves the ability to feel the emotions that come with it. We may think we are protecting ourselves from the pain, but the reality is that we are stuck in a cycle of anger and trying to justify our thoughts. The lack of sleep and racing pulse reinforces intrusive thoughts, which we now believe to be true.

Anger is an emotion that only has power if you give it power. If unaddressed, every grievance will stop you due to the shame underlying in your subconscious. This is known as toxic shame (i.e., "This bad thing happened, or I did something bad, therefore *I* am bad"). It will cause you to withdraw further, which only causes more isolationist tendencies.

CHANGING THE STORY

SPIRITUAL COGNITION
A Mindful View of the Situation

If you are not careful, the anger that's causing you to separate from others can also cause you to separate from yourself. Meditation is helpful during this stage because a mindful, introspective state can help you feel connected with something bigger than yourself. Your perspective shifts from just "me" to a sense of "we." Eventually, this helps anger's grip on you to loosen. It is important to stay connected: to yourself, to others, and to the world/higher power at large.

MENTAL FOCUS
A New Perspective to Reset Your Thoughts

"I am learning how to reconnect with myself."

QUESTIONS TO PONDER AND JOURNAL

What is the basis of your anger about what happened? What part is true and what part have you interpreted as true? What power do you feel from being angry? Do you sense any weakness in your state of anger? If so, what is it? Who around you reacts to your anger the most? Who have you pushed away due to your anger?

TOOLS TO GUIDE YOU

Write a letter to yourself containing everything you are angry about: all that feels unjust, and how each has impacted you. Put it away, then look at it again after one to two weeks. Circle all the parts in the letter that are feelings and underline the parts that are facts. What you feel at any given time comes from the lens through which you are looking at this situation. These feelings then directly impact your behavior—behavior that can keep you stuck in unwanted stages. What is one thing you are willing to change in your belief that will help you loosen anger's grip?

STAGE 8
DENIAL & ISOLATION (NUMBNESS)

IMPULSIVE REACTION
A Knee-Jerk View of the Situation

"I just want this to go away."

EMOTIONAL REACTION
The Story (Real or Imagined) You are Telling Yourself

During this stage, you may bounce back into feelings of withdrawal. Wishful thinking comes into play as you hope the pain will go away if you simply ignore it. Perhaps you daydream about reuniting with your ex, your job, a friend. You wonder, "Am I overreacting?" You may waffle between denial and anger, upset that you are having such a visceral response to the situation.

PHYSICAL REACTION
What is Happening in Your Body

With feelings of numbness, you may either be sleeping a lot or having trouble falling/staying asleep. Maybe you toss and turn in bed. The sheets feel uncomfortable because you feel uncomfortable in your own skin. The nervous system is in hyperdrive, which makes it hard to problem-solve. Due to this physical response, we can often make poor decisions, like calling your ex and even sleeping with them. Because our weak nervous system makes it hard to reflect, it is easy to have unreasonable thoughts and actions.

PSYCHOLOGICAL REACTION
What is Happening in Your Brain

It is totally normal to slip backwards and jump forwards in the healing process. We exist as multilayered humans, full of memories and emotions. When we are on a path of healing, many of these memories will be brought back into our conscious mind. This can be quite shocking, taking us back to stages of denial. You will likely want to place blame on someone or something in order to specifically excuse the situation. Not knowing where to look, you become more agitated. Do not allow these feelings to influence your relationships with others or even yourself. Do not sink into a "who needs them anyway?" mentality by cutting out loved ones.

CHANGING THE STORY

SPIRITUAL COGNITION
A Mindful View of the Situation

Be aware of yourself. You are a soul (an energy force within you) living a human experience. When things are really hard, remember that it will pass. When things are wonderful, always be in the now because even those good times will pass. The one constant is your relationship with yourself.

As you work on being consciously aware of this journey, be aware of *you*. Who are you now? Remember the exercise from Stage 2 and take another look in the mirror. Look at your eyes. Look into your eyes. See yourself. Feel your feet flat on the ground. You are here. You are here, now. If this is a past hurt you are trying to heal, pull out those pictures of yourself during this time period, the same ones that you examined during Stage 3. Look at your adolescent self. That was then. Separate who you are now from who you were in the past. Continue returning to these pictures on your healing journey through grief.

MENTAL FOCUS

A New Perspective to Reset Your Thoughts

"I can trust in my process again. One step at a time..."

QUESTIONS TO PONDER AND JOURNAL

What does trust mean to you? How was trust demonstrated to you in your childhood? Were your parents trustworthy? Did your parents trust you? Why or why not? Are there any patterns in your childhood that you see reflected in your adult life?

TOOLS TO GUIDE YOU

If you haven't already, it is time to reach out to someone you trust. Talk to them about the situation and be honest with them about your anger and other feelings. Sometimes what we need most is an audience to listen to us in order to help us work out the kinks of our emotions. If you are hesitant to speak to someone in person, try finding a safe space online with a professional mental health worker.

STAGE 9
ANGER & PARANOIA

IMPULSIVE REACTION

A Knee-Jerk View of the Situation

"What are people thinking or saying about me? How dare they. They have no idea what this is like for me."

EMOTIONAL REACTION

The Story (Real or Imagined) You are Telling Yourself

We are triggered into anger when something we had hoped for doesn't happen. It acts as a mask for our deeper pain. Anger at this stage can also come from the fact that we are upset that others are not equally upset. This level of anger can be especially infuriating because it feels like no one understands us, which in itself feels even more isolating. We can easily get lost in this stage. As frustration compounds upon itself, we feel the need to take charge—to *make* others see why they should be angry. This can lead to destructive behavior, internally or even externally.

PHYSICAL REACTION

What is Happening in Your Body

Anger results in high blood pressure, which not only impacts your physical health but also your mental health. Research has indicated that high blood pressure causes inflammation in our bodies, eventually leading to severe mental conditions such as depression.

PSYCHOLOGICAL REACTION

What is Happening in Your Brain

If we look at science, particularly quantum physics, every action has a reaction. You may be mentally lashing out and seeking revenge for the pain you feel, which often involves hurting other people. Be careful about the decisions you make when you are angry—both actions and words—because they will reflect back onto you. Revenge will not bring you peace or resolve. By dragging others into your grieving process, you will only sink yourself deeper into the pain of betrayal or disappointment. It is not uncommon to lose control of your emotions during this time but remember that you are in control of your own actions. Be mindful with each decision you make.

CHANGING THE STORY

SPIRITUAL COGNITION
A Mindful View of the Situation

Words and feelings have power. Lashing out in anger (both mentally and verbally) has an impact on your brain structure. Studies have shown that when you say mean words into water, the water structure becomes fragmented and distorted; similarly, when we use mean and aggressive language with ourselves or others, we hurt and distort our relationship with these people. Your brain is made of mostly water, after all; consider how hurtful words might influence it. This is where singing and chanting might be helpful, as the frequency of vibrations caused by each act can change our thoughts and emotions. Studies have found that chanting increases the white matter in the upper partial part of the brain, helping us to process emotional pain and situations.

MENTAL FOCUS
A New Perspective to Reset Your Thoughts

"I am not in control of my reputation, but I am in control of my character."

QUESTIONS TO PONDER AND JOURNAL

What is it about your pain or hurt from this event that leaves you feeling like you are entitled to your anger? How does this way of thinking keep you stuck? Can you acknowledge that it only feels real or true because you believe it? What would you need to change for you to start letting go of your anger? What would you have to believe instead?

TOOLS TO GUIDE YOU

- **Breath meditations.** With the support of my eldest son and his friends, I developed six beautiful prayer-meditations from the biggest religions in the world. Sit or lie down as you listen to these prayers, which are included for free with this book. Additionally, you can find my album, *Sacred Chants from World Religions*, on Spotify, Apple Music, and my own website.

- **Chanting meditations.** There are three chanting-based meditations that I have found to be highly effective. You will find these in the Tools section for download with this book. I have recommended these to clients for years due to witnessing evidence-based change in those who practice them. A free download for each of these chanting meditations is provided with this book.

STAGE 10
SELF-RIGHTEOUS ANGER

IMPULSIVE REACTION
A Knee-Jerk View of the Situation

"I deserve to be angry. I trusted them, yet they betrayed me."

EMOTIONAL REACTION
The Story (Real or Imagined) You are Telling Yourself

The deep hurt that starts to come in during this stage fuels your anger through self-righteous rhetoric. You feel you have a right to be angry; it's your prerogative. During this emotionally chaotic time, you may desire or flat out *need* to control the narrative. This is often why we drag others down with us; our insistence on sharing our story—whether true or not—asserts a sense of authority. If someone happens to share an opposing view, we feel a deep need to set them straight. We literally can't bear to hear anything else.

PHYSICAL REACTION
What is Happening in Your Body

Our body reacts to anger by raising our blood pressure. Perhaps you've heard, "I am so mad, my blood is boiling?" When we have high blood pressure, it is harder for our internal system (our mind and brain) to tolerate noncompliance. We are more likely to argue. We can't see the other side. All we see is our view, like the horses in New York City with blinders on so they don't get triggered by the traffic around them.

PSYCHOLOGICAL REACTION
What is Happening in Your Brain

In this angry state of mind, we view life through a lens of betrayal. When we hold both anger and betrayal inside, our knee-jerk reaction is one of defensiveness. This sets us up to get stuck in a loop, like a hamster in a wheel running on an endless track. It is time to set a new pattern. Stepping out of that lens of betrayal will help you get off that hamster wheel.

CHANGING THE STORY

SPIRITUAL COGNITION

A Mindful View of the Situation

Being in a relationship with our inner self means we are better able to witness our process, allowing us to make necessary changes. Otherwise, we are stuck observing ourselves from a distance, helplessly watching ourselves disappear into sinking sand. All religions and spiritual paths encourage a journey of self-discovery—and there are many different paths which you can take. Part of the journey is learning how to let go of what we believe. Embrace the idea of, "This happened to me. I will not let falsehoods become me or define me."

MENTAL FOCUS

A New Perspective to Reset Your Thoughts

"I am letting go of my story."

QUESTIONS TO PONDER AND JOURNAL

What does being emotionally aware mean to you? Have you ever noticed yourself *being* an emotion instead of *having* an emotion? This is when our emotion shows up (physically or emotionally), after which it is all we can see, feel, or act. We get lost in the emotion, then it becomes our identity. You should be able to have an emotion related to an event without it consuming all of you. The aim is to be able to recognize how a person/experience is causing you to feel an emotion without becoming that emotion.

TOOLS TO GUIDE YOU

Sit in a quiet place where you can reflect on your thoughts and feelings without any distractions. Rest your hands in your lap or on your knees. Close your eyes. Start to deeply listen to yourself: what you are feeling physically, what you are feeling emotionally, what you are thinking. Each time you notice something new, say silently or out loud, "A part of me is thinking/feeling (say what you are thinking/feeling)." Continue for three, five, or seven minutes. There is no supplementary music for this exercise because you are meant to be with yourself. If it feels horrible and makes you anxious, start with a one-minute exercise and build up your tolerance. Give it time. If it still makes you too anxious, practice with a chanting-meditation of your choice until your mind learns to slow down.

STAGE 11
ANGER & ANXIETY

IMPULSIVE REACTION

A Knee-Jerk View of the Situation

"Well, ****. Why am I still stuck? What now? I don't know what to do."

EMOTIONAL REACTION

The Story (Real or Imagined) You are Telling Yourself

As the dust settles and the anger begins to dissipate, you may start to feel fear creeping in to take its place. You may feel concerned that you are not being understood, that your story isn't being heard. From this fear, you start to enter a phase similar to mourning. This is often difficult to adjust to because it feels like admitting defeat, like the other side has "won." You become angry with life.

PHYSICAL REACTION

What is Happening in Your Body

What came first, the anger or the anxiety? We often don't know. Over time, powerful emotions lead to physical and emotional anxiety. When we experience fear and anger, our brains release a chemical called norepinephrine. In moderation, this neurotransmitter is not harmful; in fact, we need it for everyday processing. In excess, however, it can become dangerous. When we are angry, fearful, and anxious, our bodies release more norepinephrine than necessary, putting us in a fight-or-flight response. The energy of this anger causes an anxious feeling in your body. That energy has to go somewhere, so we explode and lash out at others or implode and attack ourselves.

PSYCHOLOGICAL REACTION
What is Happening in Your Brain

The mask that we put on to maintain a sense of normalcy is what keeps us stuck in the various stages of grief. Rather than being stoic, don't be afraid to talk about how disappointment is affecting you. Try not to isolate yourself from the world or from your friends by crawling into bed and sleeping off the pain. Stay physical instead. Keep moving. Remain connected to life.

Depending on the pain we experience, we may feel more or less justified in our anger. It is possible to honor this emotion without it hurting ourselves or others. Pause and honestly reflect on what you are feeling in this situation. Learn from this anger.

CHANGING THE STORY

SPIRITUAL COGNITION
A Mindful View of the Situation

Trauma is often used as an excuse not to live our lives. It is time to drop the elaborate novel you have written in your head. Confront your reality by remaining grounded. This may be uncomfortable at first because it necessitates that you sit with thoughts and emotions deep inside yourself. It forces you to ask, "Who am I? What do I live by?" These are hard questions to answer.

For example: I had a friend who had an affair. She and her husband split up. Our friend group drifted apart from her afterward because, I think, we were all confronted with similarly difficult questions. Witnessing her unhappiness made us reflect on whether we were happy in our own relationships, which fostered fear. We like living in denial of self-reflection, yet addressing emotions in such a way can help us through the stages of disappointment. It is all about being honest about yourself, to yourself.

MENTAL FOCUS

A New Perspective to Reset Your Thoughts

"I trust the process, and I am not afraid."

QUESTIONS TO PONDER AND JOURNAL

What makes you feel stuck? What makes you confused? What triggers you the most from this painful experience? What are you most afraid of? What life story are you telling yourself right now? Have you been keeping your head in the clouds or buried in the sand? Is this working for you, or do you find yourself now stagnant?

Write about where you see yourself in another week, another month, another year. Instead of dwelling on the pain, focus on your life's potential.

TOOLS TO GUIDE YOU

Sign up for something new. It could be a hobby, an exercise class, a cooking class, or art class. What matters is opening yourself up to new information, new experiences. The act of learning requires us to be more open-minded and receptive, so it helps us get out of our "angry mind" and unstuck. Whichever class you sign up for, give it at least three tries before deciding whether or not it is for you. We need some time to bypass our critical mind to really experience something new.

STAGE 12
WISHFUL THINKING & BARGAINING

IMPULSIVE REACTION
A Knee-Jerk View of the Situation

"I wish it would be how it was. Maybe if I do XYZ, everything will be fixed."

EMOTIONAL REACTION
The Story (Real or Imagined) You are Telling Yourself

Trying to bargain with yourself is another way to keep yourself enmeshed in the dysfunction of the situation. Wishing things were different by holding onto the past prevents you from truly moving forward. We fall back into withdrawal, hoping the pain will go away or that the situation will reverse itself and all will be okay again. In this stage, you are still categorizing your feelings and trying to make sense of your anger.

PHYSICAL REACTION
What is Happening in Your Body

With wishful thinking and anxiety, our blood pressure increases. Because we can't manage biases or polarized situations under this physical strain, it can be hard to make decisions. This can result in contradictory emotions, like being pissed off at an old boss yet still wanting to get your job back.

PSYCHOLOGICAL REACTION
What is Happening in Your Brain

When we start bargaining to make sense of our emotions, we suppress our physical and emotional feelings. This causes us to get stuck in our approach to the situation. Sometimes this means we get trapped at the level of emotional maturity we were in when the event occurred. For example, if we are working on healing our pain and disappointment from something that happened to us when we were seven years old, we could be operating with seven-year-old emotions inside an adult body.

CHANGING THE STORY

SPIRITUAL COGNITION
A Mindful View of the Situation

During the bargaining process, our mind is often stuck balancing contradictory emotions at the same time. In order to overcome this confusion, we need to learn how to sit with all of these emotions—while not letting any of them control you to the point where you can only see that one emotion.

MENTAL FOCUS
A New Perspective to Reset Your Thoughts

"I can hold two opposing emotions at once."

QUESTIONS TO PONDER AND JOURNAL

What are the hardest emotions for you to feel? What are they based on? What triggers these emotions? Which two emotions that feel opposed to each other, can result in you feeling stuck and/or reactive?

TOOLS TO GUIDE YOU

Learn to see and appreciate all the things and events that are opposed yet work together, such as darkness and lightness, hot and cold, love and hate. When we love someone so intensely, we can conversely match that love with anger. Practice seeing opposites around you and contemplate them, particularly how these contrasts can work in harmony.

STAGE 13
ANGER & LOW SELF-ESTEEM

IMPULSIVE REACTION
A Knee-Jerk View of the Situation

"I wish it could all be normal again."

EMOTIONAL REACTION
The Story (Real or Imagined) You are Telling Yourself

Anger and low self-esteem are difficult emotions to feel at the same time. The combination often results in feeling simultaneously lost and aggressive. Your self-esteem is fueled by this anger, so you start to beat yourself up emotionally. You may have blameful thoughts like, "What is so wrong with me that I deserve this pain?"

PHYSICAL REACTION
What is Happening in Your Body

The combination of anger and low self-esteem makes us less able to maintain physical and mental boundaries. (This may be why you feel tempted to drive by an ex's house or an old workplace.) You may not be able to recognize when to cut yourself off from certain activities, particularly if you are trying to self-medicate. At this stage, be careful not to abuse substances as an escape, such as smoking, drinking, other recreational drugs, or even food (overeating). If you feel inclined to self-harm, please reach out to a friend or licensed mental health professional immediately.

PSYCHOLOGICAL REACTION
What is Happening in Your Brain

Anger and low self-esteem are two emotions that don't work well together—or rather, they work against us *too* well. They impact each other in negative ways, compounding their effects. Anger with low self-esteem makes us aggressive and needy, while low self-esteem with anger makes us insecure with no boundaries. This becomes a back-and-forth movement of emotions, like a teeter-totter.

CHANGING THE STORY

SPIRITUAL COGNITION
A Mindful View of the Situation

It is imperative that we understand how we process our thoughts. There is a great quote in the mindfulness community that states, "Don't believe everything you think." Your thoughts only exist in your own head; they are not real, tangible objects. You can choose to think and act differently. You can easily say, "No, thank you" to the entrapment born of negative thought patterns. Remember that these emotions are happening within you; they are not *you*.

MENTAL FOCUS
A New Perspective to Reset Your Thoughts

"My life is a journey of personal choices."

QUESTIONS TO PONDER AND JOURNAL

What is your story about anger like now? What is your story about self-worth like now? How did you learn to feel this way about yourself? If you were to ask a close friend how they see you, what might they say your strengths are? What keeps you from believing them?

TOOLS TO GUIDE YOU

When we are angry and have low self-esteem, we can feel physically and emotionally paralyzed. To counteract these effects, try moving your body. As you may have noticed while traveling through these stages, there is a pattern with keeping our bodies and minds in motion. The Dalai Lama has stated, "Happiness is not something ready-made. It comes from your own actions." Find an action that creates joy: meditation, yoga, running, a new and inspiring hobby, etc.

STAGE 14
ANGER (REVENGE)

IMPULSIVE REACTION
A Knee-Jerk View of the Situation

"Karma is a *****. I hope you hurt as much as you hurt me. You are nothing without me."

EMOTIONAL REACTION
The Story (Real or Imagined) You are Telling Yourself

While we may not actually act them out, this stage often inspires vengeful thoughts. We are so angry with the other party that all we want is for them to pay for the pain they have caused. It hurts so much, making us feel justified in our revengeful anger. The old saying, "An eye for an eye" starts to sound good to us. Sadly, this attitude will only perpetuate your lingering anger, keeping you stuck in a groove of deep, untapped rage.

PHYSICAL REACTION
What is Happening in Your Body

When anger is so intense that acts of revenge are ideated, the body often experiences physical sensations such as headaches. The pounding and throbbing felt in our head and temples is such a nuisance that it reinforces our anger. While under duress from extreme emotions, our immune systems are weakened, which means we are more prone to colds and infections.

PSYCHOLOGICAL REACTION
What is Happening in Your Brain

Once you start feeling as though you no longer know who you are, you can feel resentful. You believe it isn't fair that you are being forced to change due to outside influences. The issue lies in your attachment to the situation and wanting things to be "fair," which obscures your efforts to know yourself and evolve. As I reminded my sons growing up: "Life is not equal for all."

So, how can you manage your expectations?

These are times in our lives when we are faced with our own reflection. We are forced to look at who we truly are. We weigh our values, our beliefs, our relationships. If we ignore this form of introspection, we end up living our lives in a fog of uncertainty. We lack a sense of self. We lack an identity. Regardless of what loss you have experienced, you are still you.

CHANGING THE STORY

SPIRITUAL COGNITION

A Mindful View of the Situation

I have often heard from others, "If there is a God, then why do bad things happen to good people?" This way of thinking is black and white, stemming from an unfounded idea that all cause and effect has to do with good or bad. Life is more complicated than that. It is not so much about the universe working to strike a balance for you—or, conversely, working against you—as it is about your own, individual life journey.

For example, my husband and I have worked hard to give our two sons the same upbringing, the same experiences, the same love. Despite that, I have heard both of them express the sentiment, "You love my brother more than me!" I don't believe that; yet in those moments, that was the truth, at least according to each of my sons. Whose job is it to change in this one moment? Or is it about coming together and working on seeing the situation from the other's view? Remember the chapter on the superpower of self-esteem. We view life through our own lens (which was created from our past). By applying healthy self-esteem to our lens, we are better equipped to *be* in the present moment. Good or bad, this moment will pass.

MENTAL FOCUS

A New Perspective to Reset Your Thoughts

"My grief is not my identity."

QUESTIONS TO PONDER AND JOURNAL

Are you willing to lose a part of yourself in order to maintain the life you once knew? Are you willing to lose your identity for a person or thing you have lost? Are you willing to hold onto this disappointment, this grief, in hopes that you will learn to live with this pain? When is it time for you to say, "I am more important than my anger. I am more than this pain?"

TOOLS TO GUIDE YOU

If you can, take a long walk outside in nature. Notice how everything around you is connected. If the wind blows, the leaves in the trees move. As the sun shines down, the earth is warmed. Everything impacts everything. We, as humans, have the ability to make our own choices that will cause their own ripple effect. What choice will you make on this walk? What is the next choice you will make on this journey of letting go of anger? If you hold onto anger, something will break. Are you willing to take that chance? If you let go, you will be able to see the bigger picture: a broader view that will allow you to see the next step towards healing.

■ STAGE 15 ■
BARGAINING & REVENGE

IMPULSIVE REACTION
A Knee-Jerk View of the Situation

"I don't need them. They need me. I want them to miss me, so *I* can leave *them*."

EMOTIONAL REACTION
The Story (Real or Imagined) You are Telling Yourself

Back to the bargaining stage, as you now start to play games with yourself. You give yourself compromises: "I will let go of X, but only if I get Y." You are afraid to let go. However, by tricking yourself with an ultimatum, you only sink deeper into your rut. You are manufacturing your own pain, perhaps to justify prolonged wallowing in any given emotion. It still doesn't feel fair. As long as you hold onto the event and related feelings, you will suffer.

PHYSICAL REACTION
What is Happening in Your Body

Our body feels the pressure of tumultuous emotions (such as anger) and the tentacles of reactions (such as bargaining and revenge) squeezing us. This pressure causes us to become anxious, as our hearts race and we have stress-induced panic attacks. This is detrimental to the quality of life *and* the quantity of life.

Research from the University of Michigan has found that anger and anxiety directly impact our organs and glands, which results in high blood pressure. Holding onto anger for years and years will actually shorten your life because of the stress it applies to the body. If you are interested in learning more about this subject, I talk about it extensively in my first book, *The Stressless Brain*.

PSYCHOLOGICAL REACTION

What is Happening in Your Brain

No amount of therapy or spiritual practice can single-handedly move you out of your pain. No one can make you feel any specific way, unless *you* want to let go and heal. You are in control of your own emotions; you are creating your own life story. You can get stuck in this story, its pain, the unjustness of it all. This is what I call an "emotional covenant." At some point on this healing journey, you made a pact with yourself and your pain: "I will never allow this to happen ever again." If this sounds familiar, know that you have locked yourself into a binding agreement with no room to move and grow.

When you try to bargain your way out of your experience, you will find yourself stuck in the previous chapter of your own story. In essence, you are sacrificing yourself—your own identity—to this pain. Do not admit defeat by exchanging your present needs for a past memory. You are more important than your memory. You have the untapped potential needed to be a fully realized individual, independent from the old story you are telling yourself—if only you can allow yourself to release that old story, and the pain associated with it.

CHANGING THE STORY

SPIRITUAL COGNITION

A Mindful View of the Situation

At this stage, we can begin to see how we loop together various thoughts and emotions to create our own story. We are holding onto the feeling of, "This happened to me, and there is nothing I can do about it." It is hard to not take something like that personally. Just remember that everyone is walking their own path, and it just so happens that different paths will sometimes overlap. It is not a personal attack from the universe.

Growth and healing are dependent on perspective. Only you can decide which paths you walk down and which paths you cross. I talk with clients about shifting their idea of the Self when this happens. This can only happen when we change our point of view from "life is happening to me" to "life is happening with me." You have the choice and it can be that simple.

MENTAL FOCUS

A New Perspective to Reset Your Thoughts

"I am an active participant in my life, and I have choice."

QUESTIONS TO PONDER AND JOURNAL

Write about the most painful aspects of this event and the trauma surrounding it. What is the earliest memory you have in which you felt something similar? What was so painful about that earliest memory? What agreement ("I will never" or "I will always") may you have made with yourself? What are you afraid you will lose if you let go of this "emotional covenant?"

Look for patterns in your life in which you have lived out this agreement in other situations or experiences and write them down.

TOOLS TO GUIDE YOU

Try doing everyday things differently. Drive home using a different route. Try different foods, go to a new restaurant, or try a new meal at a favorite establishment. Do a different workout routine or exercise in a new location. Try to get out of the habits in everyday life. Routine serves a purpose, but here and now, we want to avoid falling into ruts.

STAGE 16
ANGER

IMPULSIVE REACTION

A Knee-Jerk View of the Situation

"I am so angry, I could scream. I want to run away from this feeling."

EMOTIONAL REACTION

The Story (Real or Imagined) You are Telling Yourself

At this stage, our anger can become bigger than ourselves. It is unrelenting and, at times, uncontrollable. Anger can loom over our lives so much that it threatens to infiltrate our relationships with others. Wanting to take charge of the emotion, we try to make others see why they should also be angry about the situation. This can lead to unhealthy interactions—and sometimes even destructive behavior. Families have fallen apart over the need to control a narrative; loved ones have been cut out of lives and cast aside. Literal wars have started because of unrestrained rage.

PHYSICAL REACTION

What is Happening in Your Body

When we are angry, our amygdala and insula (or insular cortex) take control. Due to the takeover of the amygdala, our thinking part of the brain—the orbitofrontal cortex (OFC) and ventromedial prefrontal cortex (vmPFC)—fails to operate sufficiently. Instead of seeing cause and effect, we react to gut feelings and thoughts. This can feel disorienting, as it often leads to tunnel vision formed by the experience of pain, anger, shock, and sadness.

PSYCHOLOGICAL REACTION
What is Happening in Your Brain

Trapped in a state of fight-or-flight, we stop thinking rationally when we are angry. Instead, it is all about self-preservation—at least, to a point. Eventually, holding onto that anger hurts us. Whether we suppress it or express it, that bubbling rage locks us in a deep sadness that is hard to escape and can lead to depression. It is a confusing emotional state; the anger triggers sadness which triggers more anger, and the cycle continues. This turmoil can be passed down from generation to generation through storytelling and even through our DNA.

CHANGING THE STORY

SPIRITUAL COGNITION
A Mindful View of the Situation

A major component of yogic technique is the concept that our brain has three lenses through which we view life, also known as the Three Minds: the Negative Mind, the Positive Mind, and the Neutral Mind. When we are triggered with anger (and anxiety), our Negative Mind will thicken as we go into hyperdrive to protect ourselves. Everything we look at will be through the lens of, "Will this hurt me? Will this cause me harm?" This is when mindful meditation can be helpful; it serves as a tool to support the Three Minds working together. When they are in harmony, we are able to see through life's lenses more clearly.

MENTAL FOCUS
A New Perspective to Reset Your Thoughts

"I choose to carry my emotions with experience."

QUESTIONS TO PONDER AND JOURNAL

What about this experience will you carry with you for the rest of your life? What kind of anger or pain have you felt? Do you still carry those feelings with you? If so, how is that serving you? What kind of message can you take from the emotions you continue to harbor from this experience?

Practice seeing your trigger. What gives it fuel? Are you operating from your Young-Adult Self (meaning your reaction towards anger feels immature) or your Wise-Adult Self (the part of you which acknowledges cause and effect)? How has this trigger hurt you in the past? How is it hurting you now?

TOOLS TO GUIDE YOU

We make up stories to justify many of our emotions. The weight you give your anger can keep you locked in a cycle of triggers which can cause you to lash out, retreat into depression, and ultimately feel shameful. However, certain tools—such as meditation, yoga, and physical exercise (running, walking, dancing, swimming)—can help. By relaxing the amygdala and our thinking mind, the OFC and vmPFC start to function again. We can see cause and effect, allowing for a mindset more trusting of life.

▬ STAGE 17 ▬
BARGAINING & NUMBING

IMPULSIVE REACTION
A Knee-Jerk View of the Situation

"I am tired of feeling this way. Eh, whatever. I think I'm okay."

EMOTIONAL REACTION
The Story (Real or Imagined) You are Telling Yourself

We are so tired of thinking about this event. We are tired of carrying it around, but we still haven't really done the work of shifting our lens, viewing the event from a new perspective, or healing. We are more likely to be self-numbing with addictive behavior like drinking, drugs, sex, shopping, or mindlessly scrolling through social media.

This stage can often coincide with shame and guilt, symptoms of low self-esteem. To distract ourselves, we seek out external elements to soothe ourselves, keeping us stuck in a bind. This is called "emotional blunting," which is a way to try and protect ourselves. In actuality, it causes us to suppress everything—not only our emotions, but we also lose all of us.

PHYSICAL REACTION
What is Happening in Your Body

When in a numbing stage, we grow disenchanted with life. We lose interest in basic hygiene and healthy eating habits (often, this can lead to overindulgence). We have no desire to complete activities or socialize with others, each of which would support our healing process by maintaining good self-esteem.

PSYCHOLOGICAL REACTION
What is Happening in Your Brain

When we try to bargain to get out of our pain, it is usually because we are immature in our relationship to the situation. It feels both big and heavy, small and inconsequential, simultaneously just and unjust. This confusion can cause us to get stuck in a loop of pain and/or anger. This often happens if the event happened in our childhood or adolescence, as sometimes we get stuck in the emotional maturity that we were at the start of the abuse or situation. This can result in behavioral issues such as anger, revenge, indulgence, addiction, dissociation, manipulation, numbness, tantrums, and power struggles.

CHANGING THE STORY

SPIRITUAL COGNITION
A Mindful View of the Situation

When we are angry and/or depressed, we feel numb and believe we are separate from everything. We feel truly alone. Often, there is an element of shame associated; when we have an unhealthy sense of shame, it warps our perception of guilt from, "I am a good person who did something bad" to, "I did something bad, so I am a bad person." This is a learned behavior, something picked up when surrounded by individuals who do not empathetically respond to honest mistakes. Eventually, this mentality shifts into defensive behavior, particularly if you are already prone to anger.

MENTAL FOCUS
A New Perspective to Reset Your Thoughts

"Life is a journey of choices."

QUESTIONS TO PONDER AND JOURNAL

Write down your answers to the following questions and sit with them. It is time to be honest with yourself. If you find it difficult to answer these questions, ask someone you love and trust to help you.

- How do you numb yourself?
- What do you use to distract yourself from the reality of the situation?
- What keeps you from living life fully?
- What is your defense mode?

Write down your answers to these questions and sit with them. It is time to be honest with yourself. If you find it difficult to answer them, ask someone you love and trust to help you.

TOOLS TO GUIDE YOU

When our neurotransmitters don't work properly, we can give them extra support by taking amino acid supplements. Amino acids are protein builders that connect our neurotransmitters so that we can function at our emotional best.

Here are some aminos which help support the production of serotonin and endorphins:

- 5-hydroxytryptophan, or 5HTP (50-200mg, one to three times a day with food). Do not take if you are on any SSRI or SNRI medication.
- D-phenylalanine (500-200mg, one to three times a day with or without food). Do not confuse it for DL-phenylalanine, which has L-tyrosine. If you have melanoma, it is especially important to not mistake the two.

Always consult with your doctor before implementing any kind of supplement into your diet. Even though amino acids are naturally present in the body, it is possible to have adverse reactions. Stop taking them immediately if you experience any negative side effects.

STAGE 18
BARGAINING & NUMBING

IMPULSIVE REACTION

A Knee-Jerk View of the Situation

"It wasn't so bad. Look at how I turned out...I am better off without them."

EMOTIONAL REACTION

The Story (Real or Imagined) You are Telling Yourself

You are placing all of your bargaining chips on the table: "If I do XYZ, will I find peace?" You feel tempted to numb yourself to the pain by refusing to think about it altogether, hoping that means the deep ache will finally go away. You are so tired of feeling hurt, even though you haven't truly sat with your pain. You think if you stop being reminded of the person or thing you lost, the ache will subside.

Desperate to step out of the shadow of pain, you often wish you could turn back time to try and "make things right." However, wishing things were how they were in the past is another way of ignoring the pain, which prevents you from progressing to how things will be in the future. By blessing it and releasing it, you can set yourself free. Yet even that somehow feels like a loss. You need to start recognizing that both power and opportunity exist inside of you.

PHYSICAL REACTION

What is Happening in Your Body

During these stages of numbness and emotional blunting, you sleep more than usual. Despite sleeping a lot, you still feel like you can't get enough sleep. You are tired all the time. You feel numb. You can't differentiate between being hungry or full because you are so disconnected from your own body.

PSYCHOLOGICAL REACTION

What is Happening in Your Brain

A part of yourself has shut down, even cognitively. The burden of pain has caused so much distress, parts of your brain have ceased functioning at full capacity. Your body has entered into a self-preservation mode. When we are stuck in this stage of bargaining and numbing, we are unable to clearly see our lives and all that is happening around us. Instead, we are stuck in a world that only exists inside us. We believe our self-made realities to be the truth, and we can't bear to hear others telling us otherwise, even though they are only trying to help us.

CHANGING THE STORY

SPIRITUAL COGNITION

A Mindful View of the Situation

Eastern philosophy believes that we all have a Soul, and that our Soul is here for a human experience. We chose to come to this earthly realm with the specific purpose of experiencing life and all it has to offer. The Soul doesn't see good or bad, right or wrong; it sees everything as a whole experience. We have to be in a secure headspace to adequately process this concept because it can feel like a personal attack, as though you welcomed this feeling of pain and suffering. Try to process it with patience and grace.

MENTAL FOCUS

A New Perspective to Reset Your Thoughts

"I am more than my memories."

QUESTIONS TO PONDER AND JOURNAL

Is there a chance that life is happening around you and not happening with you? What would you need to think to shift this perspective?

What are you afraid of if you do make this perspective shift? What keeps you stuck with this perspective? From whom did you learn this?

TOOLS TO GUIDE YOU

Start working on being more connected to this planet by spending time in nature. Experience the earth. Go outside for a walk. Appreciate the warmth of sunlight and a cool breeze. Place your bare feet in grass or water. Practice this daily until you find yourself more connected to your body. Take a look at your diet, too. What are you putting into your body? Are you eating whole foods? Are you drinking plenty of water? As the saying goes, you are what you eat—so eat well and be well.

STAGE 19
DEPRESSION

IMPULSIVE REACTION
A Knee-Jerk View of the Situation

"I trusted them. How could this have happened? I am so sad. I am so depressed."

EMOTIONAL REACTION
The Story (Real or Imagined) You are Telling Yourself

The first bout of real sadness caused by this event is shocking and confusing. It slowly creeps in, leaving you feeling needy and depressed. You were already lonely, but now you also *feel* alone—not because you have isolated yourself, but because of a belief that no one loves you. Your world feels dark and gloomy, like a cloud is constantly hanging overhead. The "why's" in this stage are deep: "Why did this happen? Why me?"

PHYSICAL REACTION
What is Happening in Your Body

You have trouble falling asleep and/or staying asleep. You toss and turn all night. You lay awake in bed with your eyes open. The sheets feel too warm; they are suffocating. You feel so completely alone, physically and emotionally.

PSYCHOLOGICAL REACTION
What is Happening in Your Brain

Loss is a natural occurrence in life. Don't feel ashamed to live in your sadness for a while. You may feel lonely or confused because you're not sure what the future holds. This is a normal part of the process. You have just experienced a life-changing hardship that left you with a lot of pain, a lot of disappointment, and you are figuring it out. But remember that this, too, shall pass.

For the time being, it is important to learn how to be with your emotions. For some, this may require going to therapy. If you find you need additional assistance, don't hesitate to reach out to a mental health professional. A therapist can help you understand what your emotions are and how they are serving you. They will help pull the light out from inside you so that you can continue on your healing journey with more guidance.

CHANGING THE STORY

SPIRITUAL COGNITION

A Mindful View of the Situation

When we feel alone, we can feel lost. We feel the vastness of the world, and yet we feel so isolated within our own existence. This woe-is-me mentality is a pity party we like to throw for ourselves when we are disconnected from the larger universe. It is important to forge a connection to a higher source, energy, or God-entity (whatever that means to you). In doing so, we come to better understand our place in the universe. We can find peace in the interconnectedness of the collective consciousness.

MENTAL FOCUS

A New Perspective to Reset Your Thoughts

"No matter what darkness surrounds me, there is a light inside of me."

QUESTIONS TO PONDER AND JOURNAL

As you enter the dark cave of depression, reassure yourself that you are carrying a light that will help guide you. This inner light is something that serves you by giving you hope and support. When we are depressed, we feel isolated and alone, so we need some kind of connection beyond ourselves. As I mentioned in Chapter 5, it helps to have faith. Practice connecting to this inner light, whatever that means to you. It can be as simple as going outside and standing in the sun. Feel the warmth of the rays and breathe deeply into your body, bringing that warmth inside yourself. Take special note of how this sensation feels to you.

Where do you sense this light is inside you? What color is it, and what does that mean to you? When did you first learn of your light? How can your previous experience with it help you through your hardship now?

TOOLS TO GUIDE YOU

Do you want this event, this situation, this memory to be the end of your life or the beginning of your life? Will your life stop here, or do you want to learn the lesson that this experience offers so that you can move onward—and thrive? Allow these questions to be seeds of thoughts as you consider the possibility of growth. The choice is yours.

■ STAGE 20 ■
DEPRESSION

IMPULSIVE REACTION
A Knee-Jerk View of the Situation

"I wish this would stop. But what if it doesn't?"

EMOTIONAL REACTION
The Story (Real or Imagined) You are Telling Yourself

You may find that you are holding onto past stories which inflame your emotions, further shackling yourself to your depressive state. Once again, you may feel stuck. The story you are crafting in your head is shifting; you may even be turning yourself into the villain. If your experience involves another party, they might become the victim.

PHYSICAL REACTION
What is Happening in Your Body

Emotions impact our bodies and reinforce fictitious stories in our heads. They feel so immediate and real, it is hard for the body to differentiate the truth from these stories. It is like dying from a broken heart—and it can happen. When we are feeling depressed, our blood vessels constrict which can lead to cardiovascular disease.

PSYCHOLOGICAL REACTION
What is Happening in Your Brain

If you find you are stuck in the same old bad story of your past, it is because your brain does not have enough creativity to think outside of the box. This doesn't mean that you are incapable of doing so; often, we get stuck simply because overstimulation paralyzes us. Creativity lives within all of us, but negative thought patterns will block you from tapping into that frequency.

CHANGING THE STORY

SPIRITUAL COGNITION

A Mindful View of the Situation

How you live your life at this stage is a choice that only you can make. Try to celebrate the little victories you accomplish on a daily basis, no matter how small. Feel gratitude towards having running water in the house and a bed to sleep in at night. Even though the situation is painful, you can be thankful for supportive family and friends. Treat yourself by going to the grocery store and purchasing food to enjoy. Even if the glass is only 10 percent full, at least it is not empty. Even though the pain is real, you are surviving.

MENTAL FOCUS

A New Perspective to Reset Your Thoughts

"I will acknowledge my sadness, knowing that my sadness does not define me."

QUESTIONS TO PONDER AND JOURNAL

Is it easy or hard for you to feel sadness? Why do you think this is? Do you find that you want to resist the feeling of sadness? What happened in your past to make you believe that it is unacceptable to feel sad? What can you do in order to acknowledge any suppressed sadness, fear, or lingering anger? How will you honor your emotions?

TOOLS TO GUIDE YOU

Meditation can allow you to cut through negatively influential thought patterns, especially the harmful ones that have no basis in reality. Remember that your thoughts are not tactile; they cannot physically harm you. They have no power unless you give them power, so refrain from allowing negative words and thoughts to plant themselves in your mind.

═══ STAGE 21 ═══
DEPRESSION

IMPULSIVE REACTION
A Knee-Jerk View of the Situation

"I can't stop crying. I feel such a deep sadness."

EMOTIONAL REACTION
The Story (Real or Imagined) You are Telling Yourself

At this stage, you are crying a lot. You don't want to get out of bed. When you do try to involve yourself in society, everything feels slow. You think people are looking at you oddly, like they're judging you. Even though friends and family are trying to reassure you that things will get better and you will be fine, you don't believe it because they can't possibly understand how painful this is for you. You feel such deep pain and despair, you are almost embarrassed to tell people how sad you are. Sometimes you don't want to be here; you wish you could become invisible if it meant your feelings would also disappear.

PHYSICAL REACTION
What is Happening in Your Body

When experiencing deep sadness or depression, our weight can fluctuate. We lean towards the extremes of not eating enough or eating too much. We are so disconnected from our bodies that we can't register cues of hunger and fullness. Our digestive system is impacted by the sluggish energy of this state, so there are often bowel complications. In addition to troubled eating habits, we may have diarrhea or constipation.

PSYCHOLOGICAL REACTION

What is Happening in Your Brain

Mourning is part of depression. This stage can take a day, a month, a year—sometimes even a lifetime. Only you can determine how long you remain in this stage. That isn't to say you should rush through your pain, however—mourning is an essential component to healing. Like anger, this depressive state is not something you can sidestep. You have to process sadness and the stories you carry with it.

CHANGING THE STORY

SPIRITUAL COGNITION

A Mindful View of the Situation

Depression can be a deep, dark hole that feels inescapable. This is why it is important to find your internal light; something to help lead you out and away from the darkness. Sometimes that light is merely a pinhole, but it is still there. If there is a way in, then there is a way out. Keep your eyes on that light.

MENTAL FOCUS

A New Perspective to Reset Your Thoughts

"Even though the pain is real, I am a survivor."

QUESTIONS TO PONDER AND JOURNAL

What are you most sad about? What does your sadness feel like to you? How do you feel it in your body? How did you learn how to handle sadness? Do you hide sadness, or do you display it to others?

TOOLS TO GUIDE YOU

Find some time to sit in solitude with yourself. Allow your sadness/ depression/grief to wash over you. Allow yourself to feel these emotions in your entire body. Acknowledge how this particular stage looks to you and envision how it will look once it passes. You must learn how to steep in your own emotions in order to fully understand and process them. It is not always a quick process, and that's fine. Take it one day at a time.

STAGE 22
DEPRESSION

IMPULSIVE REACTION
A Knee-Jerk View of the Situation

"I don't want to be alone."

EMOTIONAL REACTION
The Story (Real or Imagined) You are Telling Yourself

During this stage of depression, you may start finding yourself feeling needy. Loneliness is much more compounded. Instead of the earlier feelings of isolation, you may now wish more people were reaching out to you—and if they aren't, you may confuse their distance with neglect. You may start to wonder if something is wrong with you, that maybe this is your fault.

PHYSICAL REACTION
What is Happening in Your Body

Neediness can manifest itself as anxiety in the body, which results in vague aches like joint or limb pain. You might notice a tight stomach or that you are clenching your jaw a lot. Anxiety can also cause a buzzing energy throughout the body, almost like having too much caffeine. It doesn't feel good. The sensations are exhausting and can make us even more depressed; for some, the chronic exhaustion can lead to anger. Our immune system is weakened because it is working on managing a flight-or-fight response to our emotional thoughts, regardless of whether they have any rational basis.

PSYCHOLOGICAL REACTION

What is Happening in Your Brain

It is easy to place blame on ourselves when we are in a vulnerable state of mind. Avoid making up stories and faulting yourself for the situation. It will be difficult. The more historical trauma you are working through, the harder it will be to let go of old thinking habits. Humans are masterminds at suppressing emotions; by masking them, we give ourselves the illusion of strength. Heal your trauma, and your lifestyle will start to follow suit. Your level of healthy self-esteem and emotional maturity directly affects the level at which you are able to connect to and address your needs.

CHANGING THE STORY

SPIRITUAL COGNITION

A Mindful View of the Situation

At this stage, we are still working on our connection to a higher source. Over my 23 years of working with clients, I have noticed that those who have some kind of faith in a higher power or source are more readily able to process pain. Don't get me wrong: if the faith pendulum swings too far left or too far right, you will be off-balance. For example, if you believe in nothing, you may feel like you are messing up your one shot at life. On the opposite end of the spectrum, if you are devoutly religious, you may believe that God is out to punish you because you are sinful. Work on being somewhere in the middle, where you simply feel an energetic connection to something greater than yourself. You have free will and the ability to make choices to benefit yourself. You just need to decide to do the work.

MENTAL FOCUS

A New Perspective to Reset Your Thoughts

"I will keep walking down the path, even if it is sometimes sideways."

QUESTIONS TO PONDER AND JOURNAL

What were your beliefs as a child? What did/does your family believe? What support can you build inside yourself that will help you feel more anchored in life? What can you connect to which cannot be heard, seen, or touched? If there is nothing, what keeps you disconnected from a higher source?

TOOLS TO GUIDE YOU

Take some time to read about the different faiths in the world. Lie down somewhere comfortable (on your bed, couch, or floor) and cover your body with a blanket. Listen to prayers or hymns from different faiths, and feel their words move through your body. You don't need to believe the words, necessarily; you are working on feeling their energy inside you. These are tools to bring you closer to your own Soul.

If you would prefer a more physical assignment, try going outside. Feel the sun on your face. Feel the rain on your face. Feel the grass and dirt under your feet. When you die, will your body return to the earth? Consider that all of this organic material—including yourself—came from the same source. Feel the connection within that truth.

■ STAGE 23 ■
DEPRESSION & WONDERING

IMPULSIVE REACTION
A Knee-Jerk View of the Situation

"I am still so down. I hope this will start to change soon..."

EMOTIONAL REACTION
The Story (Real or Imagined) You are Telling Yourself

Mourning is a huge component of healing, and it is a process that can take a lifetime. Whether this is a long or short stage is dependent on you and you alone. As you mull over things in this depressive state, you may start to wonder, "Surely there is a way through this? Others have had something traumatic happen to them and lived to see the other side." This is a positive—you are starting to have a little hope—but there are still layers to this grief you have yet to explore.

PHYSICAL REACTION
What is Happening in Your Body

It can sometimes take a while for our physical symptoms to get better. It won't happen overnight, especially if you have been feeling angry or depressed for months or even years. Just like losing weight, we need to put in a lot of routine work before we notice any changes. Some of the first physical signs of change from depression is that we start to care more about our hygiene, the food we eat, and our water intake. There is a desire to feel something different from what you have been feeling, which means you want to take care of yourself more.

PSYCHOLOGICAL REACTION

What is Happening in Your Brain

When we get stuck in the depression stage, we often lose the concept of loving ourselves. The grief that we are enduring—especially if it involves giving away our power to a lost relationship—sets us up to become needy individuals. We may feel desperate for someone or something to fill the void in our life. If this cannot or does not happen for whatever reason, we become depressed. However, we have the power to choose.

You can make the decision to let go of the old story—the disappointment, the anger, the pain—or you can decide to fall into a self-defeating role of dependence on others. You will only truly feel fully liberated once you can help yourself.

CHANGING THE STORY

SPIRITUAL COGNITION

A Mindful View of the Situation

Find your own voice—literally. Singing or chanting hymns helps to open the heart center, which encourages us to open our creative self. By opening up, we are more readily able to break the habit of holding onto past pain. We need to be able to locate where our sadness is before we can release it. You can perform this activity with a friend or in a group, but you should also try practicing on your own to avoid being reliant on others.

MENTAL FOCUS

A New Perspective to Reset Your Thoughts

"I can only arrive at my destination once I know where I want to go."

QUESTIONS TO PONDER AND JOURNAL

It is normal to feel sad, especially after a traumatic event, but you cannot let emotion overrun your life. Depression can become a dark hole with seemingly no way out. Think of that light inside you, which you addressed during Stage 19. Continue using it as a guide. How can you honor your sadness without being stuck in depression?

TOOLS TO GUIDE YOU

If there is a way in, there must be a way out. Likewise, there is always a way to remove yourself from the dark hole of depression.

Work on your self-care. If you have fallen behind on your hygiene, enjoy a nice bath. If your diet has been lackluster, enjoy a meal consisting of whole foods. If you have been isolated from others, enjoy an evening out with friends. Work on making small changes every three to four days. Build on your progress. Be gentle with yourself. It takes time for a wound to heal.

STAGE 24
DEPRESSION & WONDERING

IMPULSIVE REACTION
A Knee-Jerk View of the Situation

"I was sad today, but it wasn't the only thing I felt. I can see more of life now."

EMOTIONAL REACTION
The Story (Real or Imagined) You are Telling Yourself

You are noticing that you are not sad or depressed all the time. You are feeling lighter and more curious again. You are able to laugh more easily. Slowly, you are starting to distance yourself from the event, now viewing it as something that impacted you—but not something that defines you. You are feeling some stirrings of creativity.

PHYSICAL REACTION
What is Happening in Your Body

You may notice that you are starting to have more energy. Your thoughts are clearer, and you can problem-solve again.

PSYCHOLOGICAL REACTION
What is Happening in Your Brain

Our level of emotional maturity and healthy self-esteem both affect our ability to handle our needs, especially in relation to dramatic and/or traumatic events. You have the power to heal your trauma by severing your tie to grief. If you don't let go of the story, you will fall into a self-defeating role (either being too dependent on others or becoming too independent). You may also experience helper syndrome, in which you only feel liberated when you can help liberate someone else. Focus on healing your pain first, then you can reach out to others.

CHANGING THE STORY

SPIRITUAL COGNITION
A Mindful View of the Situation

Eastern philosophy suggests that we each have a magnetic field around us called an aura. This energy field can impact how we feel about ourselves, which then influences how we live our lives. Auras are malleable and can even absorb energy from other people, especially when the aura is weak. (Think of the movie *Ghostbusters* and how a ghost moving through a person would leave slime on them.) To have a strong aura, we have to find personal meaning. This can't simply be "happiness," as happiness comes out of finding a specific purpose in life and following through with it. What is your purpose?

MENTAL FOCUS
A New Perspective to Reset Your Thoughts

"I let go of my attachments because I don't want them to have power over me."

QUESTIONS TO PONDER AND JOURNAL

Notice your inner and outer boundaries. Start to redefine them. If it helps, draw a picture of yourself (a stick person is fine) or use a photograph of yourself as a visual aid. Draw two circles around yourself. In each circle, write what your inner boundaries and your outer boundaries look like to you. Add more to these circles as you learn more about yourself.

TOOLS TO GUIDE YOU

Sit in a chair or on the floor on your heels. Bring your palms together with your fingers intertwined (a *mudra*—or yoga hand position—known as Venus Lock), keeping your arms straight and elbows locked. Inhale as you raise your arms up, then exhale as you bring them back down. Continue for 3–5 minutes.

This yogic movement clears out your aura and releases excess energy. By strengthening your aura, you can feel more confident in yourself. The boundaries required to protect and deflect in your life will be more easily defined, and you will be able to see exactly how you process your thoughts and feelings. You will be able to view the reality of the situation with more clarity and insight. Facing the truth is the beginning of a happier life.

STAGE 25
ACCEPTANCE
(WONDERING & HOPE)

IMPULSIVE REACTION
A Knee-Jerk View of the Situation

"Wow, I haven't thought about this pain in days. I am starting to think this can pass. I want to find a way to move on."

EMOTIONAL REACTION
The Story (Real or Imagined) You are Telling Yourself

A new day has begun, and it is intense and wonderful—because it feels hopeful. You feel open and free. You are thriving. When we let go of our lingering connection to pain, we create space for new blessings to come into our lives. It is time to reset your goals, your desires, your faith.

PHYSICAL REACTION
What is Happening in Your Body

You are noticing physical cues in your body and recognizing your needs, whether it is sleep, food, or hygiene. You are no longer numb. You can feel coldness, hotness, hunger, thirst, tiredness—and you're adjusting your routine(s) accordingly. You are starting to feel connected to others again; you finally see how they can also have needs and wants.

PSYCHOLOGICAL REACTION
What is Happening in Your Brain

To truly drop the old pain, you must have the courage to create a new story for yourself. This will involve parts of the old story, but only the parts from which you have learned a lesson. If you still feel remnants of anger, embrace those remnants and turn them into determination instead. This will give you the motivation to let go of the disappointment and reconnect with yourself.

CHANGING THE STORY

SPIRITUAL COGNITION
A Mindful View of the Situation

My relationship to my identity, my Self, was strengthened through the use of meditation. It opened me up to self-discovery by teaching me how to be in a deliberate relationship with myself. During meditation, you learn to sit with your thoughts and your feelings; you practice being present in your body and mind.

MENTAL FOCUS
A New Perspective to Reset Your Thoughts

"My happiness is a choice."

QUESTIONS TO PONDER AND JOURNAL

The universe often has bigger plans for us than we realize. It is more than "good vibes"; it is a power within us to manifest the big dreams we harbor. What could enter into your life as a result of letting go of this old pain? Be detailed with exactly what kind of possibilities you envision within your life. At the end of your answer, write, "...or better."

TOOLS TO GUIDE YOU

If you haven't already, clean out all that is old in relation to this disappointment. It is time to let go—not just of emotional attachments, but of tactile items as well. Letting go of these objects is another form of letting go of the experience.

STAGE 26
ACCEPTANCE

IMPULSIVE REACTION
A Knee-Jerk View of the Situation

"Just because something bad happened to me doesn't mean it happened because *I'm* bad. This event does not define me. I am more than this event."

EMOTIONAL REACTION
The Story (Real or Imagined) You are Telling Yourself

You are starting to realize and accept that happiness is a choice. By releasing the old story (your relationship, the abuse, false beliefs), you are now more able to live in the present moment. Perhaps you have finally taken your anger and/or sadness and molded it into determination. Permit yourself compassion and grace as you evolve beyond the event. It takes courage and creativity to let go.

PHYSICAL REACTION
What is Happening in Your Body

Since you have reconnected to yourself, you have noticed that both your heart rate and your blood pressure are normalizing. You are able to sleep restfully and eat healthily because you are more connected to your body's needs.

PSYCHOLOGICAL REACTION
What is Happening in Your Brain

When something is removed (for example, the drama and/or trauma you have experienced), there is a new space left behind, a void that can instead be filled with something beneficial. Think of it like plucking weeds so your flowers can flourish, instead of being suppressed by invasive plants. It may be difficult but let go of those attachments that are not serving you. Once you do, you can attract new growth.

CHANGING THE STORY

SPIRITUAL COGNITION

A Mindful View of the Situation

We have invisible cords that tie us to our pain. Acknowledging these cords is the first step in being able to remove them. The next step is blessing the situation so that you can finally work on forgiveness. This is an essential step in letting go. There can often be thousands of cords, depending on the layers of trauma (real or imagined). Be patient as you work through them.

MENTAL FOCUS

A New Perspective to Reset Your Thoughts

"My power is compassion and grace."

QUESTIONS TO PONDER AND JOURNAL

In your head, what agreement or promise did you make to those who hurt you? How did this feeling resonate in your body? Do you feel as though it is time to let those go? Why or why not?

If applicable, do you feel it is time to forgive yourself? Why or why not? What else would need to happen in order for you to fully release yourself from this disappointment?

TOOLS TO GUIDE YOU

Read through the journal entries you have written throughout this healing journey. Consider all the emotions you have felt thus far and spend time sitting with each one. Try to make some kind of art piece with these emotions; invoke the transformation you have undergone and apply it to a new creation. You may choose to destroy the artwork after to release those emotions, if you feel it may benefit your emotional state in relation to this event.

═ STAGE 27 ═
ACCEPTANCE

IMPULSIVE REACTION

A Knee-Jerk View of the Situation

"It is okay that I can't control the past; it is the past. Now I can look forward to the future. Who do I want to be? I got this!"

EMOTIONAL REACTION

The Story (Real or Imagined) You are Telling Yourself

You are letting go of control, internally and externally. You find yourself blessing the situation—including any person(s) involved—so that you can set yourself free. This energy builds upon itself, gaining momentum and strength. Let it propel you forward. You are choosing to live *your* life. It is time for you to choose you. A new chapter is beginning.

PHYSICAL REACTION

What is Happening in Your Body

You are able to notice new feelings as they enter into your body—but you are able to sit with these feelings instead of being triggered by them. You feel connected to your Wise-Adult Self.

PSYCHOLOGICAL REACTION

What is Happening in Your Brain

It is time to reset your body and mind. Think of this process like eating: we only want our bodies to absorb the nutrients and dispose of the trash. Similarly, our experience with disappointment has parts that are lessons and parts that are junk. Purge your system and focus on new dreams, desires, doctrines. What goals do you have for yourself? Your body? Your career? Your health? Your friendships? Your spirituality?

CHANGING THE STORY

SPIRITUAL COGNITION
A Mindful View of the Situation

The four steps to happiness should include gratitude, exercise, sleep, and meditation. How you approach each step is up to you. You can start small, like spending five minutes exercising and writing down three things for which you are thankful. Display your plan by hanging it on your bathroom mirror or a fridge so you can continually reference it throughout the day. Tell your friends and family about your plan; this will help you manifest it by holding yourself accountable.

MENTAL FOCUS
A New Perspective to Reset Your Thoughts

"I relate to who I am rather than what happens to me. How I relate to the event is more important than the event itself."

QUESTIONS TO PONDER AND JOURNAL

What are some of your personal strengths? What areas in your life could use some attention or energy? Where do you see yourself in three, five, and seven years from now?

Write down different components that make up your life (like self-esteem, health, hobbies, career, spirituality, friendships, community relationships). Evaluate how they each impact your life positively. Revisit this list a couple of times a year.

TOOLS TO GUIDE YOU

What habits will you practice daily, weekly, and monthly to maintain this place of acceptance? Remember that acceptance does not mean you are saying what happened to you was acceptable. Rather, you are saying, "What happened to me does not define me." Acceptance means you have built a relationship with yourself and all the parts within you—everything from your wounded childhood parts to your healthy self-esteem.

STAGE 28
EXPANDED SELF-WORTH

IMPULSIVE REACTION
A Knee-Jerk View of the Situation

"I won't give away my power anymore."

EMOTIONAL REACTION
The Story (Real or Imagined) You are Telling Yourself

You are learning to view the growth potential from this bad experience and categorize it as a useful lesson. It is important to make this distinction so that you can recognize the value of the experience—and to release the toxic parts. It takes a lot of courage and grit to do this work. No one can do it for you, so the experience helps build empowerment within your own self. You are learning this lesson. You are seeing the silver lining.

PHYSICAL REACTION
What is Happening in Your Body

Exercise is all about being in the moment. How you exercise doesn't matter; just get up and move your body. This will allow blood (and energy) to flow through you, creating an internal sense of healing. On the opposite end of the spectrum, don't forget to sleep! A good night's rest boosts your immune system. Both will allow you to live in a place of healthy self-esteem, being present in your life. You are finally more in tune with yourself.

PSYCHOLOGICAL REACTION
What is Happening in Your Brain

Gratitude is a big aspect when it comes to education of the Self. It allows us to appreciate all that we already have without constant pressure to seek out something more. We are a culture that operates on always wanting newness; it is built into our society's structure. However, nothing grounds us more than being thankful for our blessings. Gratitude allows us to be more present in the here and now.

CHANGING THE STORY

SPIRITUAL COGNITION

A Mindful View of the Situation

You have value not because of what you do, what you have, who you know, or what you have achieved. You have value because of who you are. You are a unique individual, a Soul living a human experience. There will be hardships and painful experiences on this journey, and you will make some (or even a lot of) mistakes as you travel down your life's path—but those mistakes are not you. You always have choice in everything you do or say. You are not a victim. You are not a villain. You are a human being.

MENTAL FOCUS

A New Perspective to Reset Your Thoughts

"I take responsibility for how I feel."

QUESTIONS TO PONDER AND JOURNAL

Make a list of all the different kinds of disappointment you have experienced, then make another listing all the blessings in your life. Pick a few disappointments and blessings from each list and expand on how they make you feel. Faced with these lists, it's easier to see what you can let go of and what you should hold onto, with gratitude. As you go through each disappointment, say out loud, "God bless (disappointment); I let go of my attachment," then release the pain associated with it. If you don't resonate with the word "God," you can just say, "Bless (disappointment); I let go of my attachment."

TOOLS TO GUIDE YOU

Life collectively happens and we, as individuals, are simply one part of it. We all exist within our own story, which is then projected onto the masses. For example, when someone unknowingly cuts us off on the road, we create a narrative about that person. Even though they have no idea who we are, we take the act personally as though they deliberately intended to harm us. If someone dumps us, we believe that they did it solely to inflict pain on us, even if they had their own sensible reasons for the break-up.

Trauma will only haunt us for as long as we allow it. Some pain can be so unbelievable and excruciating that it can seem like there is no way through to the other side. The things that other people have said or done to us are so cruel, the hurt has left a scar. But even though the event happened to you, you have a choice in how it impacts you now, in how you continue to carry it in your life moving forward. And that is the trick: to move forward.

Be gentle with yourself. If you have some anger to work through, please get that anger out. If you have deep sadness, express it. Release it and let it go. Take a step forward. Leave the pain behind. I know you can do this, because I have, too.

━━━ STAGE 29 ━━━
GREATER HAPPINESS

IMPULSIVE REACTION

A Knee-Jerk View of the Situation

"This is my life. I am going to live it fully."

EMOTIONAL REACTION

The Story (Real or Imagined) You are Telling Yourself

Your mind is finally relaxed. You can think of upsetting memories related to this painful event and not emotionally spiral. You are able to look at the past disappointment while still progressing forward. Overall, your responses aren't irrational reactions. You are thoughtful. You are mindful. You view yourself with warm regards and high contentment.

PHYSICAL REACTION

What is Happening in Your Body

When the body is in sync with the mind and spirit, it works like a finely tuned instrument. We may still need to tighten the strings once in a while, but all the different parts inside us are communicating and working together. Many healers say that when we support our body, it forges its own path to a self-healing journey, whether it is physical or emotional. It is all about putting in the work and giving our bodies that support.

PSYCHOLOGICAL REACTION

What is Happening in Your Brain

Although it felt impossible in the thick of our journey through grief, we have learned to extract goodness even from the darkest times in our lives. With mindfulness, we can separate what is beneficial to us from the toxicity of the situation. In order to achieve this, we must be able to have a conversation with our Self about our true feelings, especially in relation to our disappointment. This creates inner strength.

CHANGING THE STORY

SPIRITUAL COGNITION

A Mindful View of the Situation

From a spiritual view, greater happiness is about connecting our human experience with our Soul's experience. It is all about responding to life rather than reacting to it. Our experiences may cause us to have strong emotions that impact us, of course, but we won't make up stories about it. We won't give reasons as to why it "should" be this way or that way. Happiness is about being present and open and secure, a state of mind which breeds contentment.

MENTAL FOCUS

A New Perspective to Reset Your Thoughts

"I am comfortable with my Self. I can handle my emotions."

QUESTIONS TO PONDER AND JOURNAL

What does happiness mean to you? How does it feel emotionally? Physically? Spiritually? Sexually? How can you strengthen your idea of happiness? What can you do to manifest this in your life? How can you apply these feelings to other areas of your life, such as a relationship, a job, and/or creative endeavors?

TOOLS TO GUIDE YOU

If you haven't already, create a daily or weekly ritual or routine that works as a filter to help you process life and all its unexpected events. This can be any one of a variety of activities: meditation, exercise, church or prayer, experiencing nature, singing or chanting, laughing, even carving out a moment for yourself to cry. Utilize whatever tools you need for you to reconnect with your inner Self.

━━━━ STAGE 30 ━━━━
PRESENT WITH THE SELF

IMPULSIVE REACTION

A Knee-Jerk View of the Situation

"I am now free from the story and inner belief. I feel more connected to my purpose."

EMOTIONAL REACTION

The Story (Real or Imagined) You are Telling Yourself

You acknowledge the past and can see through it; it no longer has control over you. You are able to let go of the stories about this event that you once told yourself and others. Your story in general has shifted. You feel closer to those around you and to yourself. You are less reactive, less angry. If you are angry, there is a purpose behind it—it has not become your new story and/or identity. You are less depressed. You are able to be in the moment and to experience it without any emotion taking over all of you.

PHYSICAL REACTION

What is Happening in Your Body

Physically and emotionally, your body is relaxed. You can think about upsetting memories and not have a physical reaction. You can be reminded of the painful event and not spiral into reactive emotions, like anger or fear. You have more physical and emotional energy, also known as vitality. Life is more colorful, brighter. Food tastes better. You experience life more fully, with all of your senses.

PSYCHOLOGICAL REACTION

What is Happening in Your Brain

There is an overall ease in living at this final stage of grief. You are able to acknowledge your past pain while maintaining your journey forward. This is because of vitality, a personal energy which carries you effortlessly through life. You may feel like you are floating in your body and mind, a sensation that allows you to take each moment as it comes. You feel yourself going with the flow. You exist in the now.

CHANGING THE STORY

SPIRITUAL COGNITION

A Mindful View of the Situation

To have vitality is to have an open energy flow. This gives us more focus, creativity, insight, intuition, and presence. It is a state in which we have the energy and courage of an 18-year-old and the wisdom and insight of an 80-year-old. Although this sounds unachievable, it is possible to get close to the ideal by connecting the mind, body, and spirit together.

MENTAL FOCUS

A New Perspective to Reset Your Thoughts

"All is what all is. Peace is in and around me."

QUESTIONS TO PONDER AND JOURNAL

What was (or still is) the light that guided you to the end of this tunnel of darkness? What is the lesson in this experience that helped you grow the most? What from this situation will you keep, and what parts will you let go? How can you apply this experience and what you learned from it to future life shake-ups?

TOOLS TO GUIDE YOU

To keep you present with the Self and to maintain your vitality, you have to continue to put in the work. Think of it like exercise: we can't stop training once we achieve the body we want, otherwise we'll fall out of shape again. What is your commitment to yourself to maintain vitality? What is your roadmap towards contentment? Write it down and follow it!

Here are some great ways to get started:

- Be courageous
- Dream big
- Drink plenty of water
- Eat a healthy diet
- Find your purpose
- Have compassion
- Let go of your past pain
- Love openly
- Maintain good sleeping habits
- Meditate
- Soak up the sun
- Walk daily

CHAPTER 8

MOVING BEYOND
THE PAIN

CONGRATULATIONS! YOU DID IT.

You set aside the time and space necessary to progress through the stages of disappointment. *You* took this time for yourself, for your growth, and for your healing. We often underestimate this achievement, as though "just doing the work" is the easiest part of the process. In truth, deciding that you need to do something—and then actually starting yourself on the path—is the hardest part. Self-initiation, the personal drive to put in the work, is key. So many of us never move past that threshold, but you did.

The journey from here will vary for each person. Everyone processes things differently: the event itself, the level of grief, the time it takes, the degree of self-reflection… And that's only the beginning. What does true healing look like? How and when does it happen? What happens after, if there *is* such a thing as an after? There is no single path for all, as we are all unique. This means that you may want or need to revisit some of the stages as you continue assessing your feelings, thoughts, and/or interpretations of your disappointment.

You may also find that you need routine maintenance. Sometimes we can work through an event only for it to resurface in a month, a year, or even 10 years; out of the blue, something triggers an old memory and the pain associated with it. The human experience is a journey with many stops and starts, and sometimes even resets but it is a journey without end, so long as you keep moving forward.

The acceptance of disappointment (including the pain and grief associated with the event) can, ironically, be a trigger for many. Clients and friends have wondered to me, "How can I possibly come to a place of 'acceptance?' This horrible situation impacted my life so much. It isn't right to be 'okay' with it." What I tell them is that "acceptance" does not mean "approval." You don't need to consent to or forgive the situation for the negative impact it has had on your life. Instead, acceptance means that you have come to a place where you acknowledge the disappointment while leaning into the potential to change your perspective about it. You see the growth mindset and accept the journey.

I am reminded of the inspiring story of hockey player Henrik Lundqvist, shared in the Netflix documentary *Open Heart* (2023). Lundqvist grew up in Sweden with his twin brother and has maintained a deep love for hockey his whole life. He became one of the great goaltenders in the NHL, playing for the New York Rangers. After becoming a free agent, he signed a new contract to become the Washington Capitals' new goalie.

However, during a routine physical, it was discovered that he had an irregular heartbeat (caused by pericarditis) and needed to undergo open-heart surgery. Despite the heart condition, Lundqvist's intention was always to return to the NHL and continue playing hockey. His dream, of course, was to win himself the Stanley Cup—the highest achievement of any NHL player.

Unfortunately, Lundqvist suffered complications from his surgery that effectively ended his hockey career. In the documentary, you can witness his journey as he navigates the release of his dream: the disappointment, the anger, and then acceptance. "To walk away from something you love doing your entire life…some people walk away when they are tired of it. They don't like it at all. I still love it. There was definitely sadness in that," Lundqvist shares in the film. "When I look forward to what's next, I think the goal is to have a different experience. I feel joy."

His beautiful words touched my heart. This reflection of his journey—the sadness, pain, wishful thinking, acceptance, and finally coming to peace with the situation—is a perfect example of the 'art of disappointment.' Lundqvist was able to shift his desire of what he wanted in a profound way, creating a path to the next stage of his life. He let go of his attachment and found a new purpose.

We are all wired differently; that is part of what makes life so rich and beautiful, even as it creates unique challenges. I think of my two sons and how they are so distinct from one another. They may have been raised by both my husband and me, and they certainly look a lot alike, but they are each their own unique selves. They process hurt, pain, and sadness differently. They react out of anger differently. They love differently. Therefore, they will heal differently—which is why the art of healing disappointment is so challenging, yet equally necessary and rewarding. I wouldn't want my sons to be any other way. I love their individuality and will always celebrate it. So, too, should you love and celebrate your individuality. It doesn't matter if your path is longer, your progress slower, your stops more frequent. What matters is that you keep moving towards a better relationship with yourself.

Hopefully, in reading this book you have learned some ways to acknowledge your own personal qualities. Keep appreciating them. Embrace your own superpowers. Have faith in them and in your potential. Use your gifts to paint yourself a better, more beautiful tomorrow. You are a master in the art of disappointment. You are the master of your life.

FREE DIGITAL
DOWNLOADS OF
MEDITATION MUSIC

FOR SOME, MANTRA MUSIC can elevate their meditative experience. I hope you find the songs helpful and enjoyable. With the purchase of this book, you can enjoy complimentary downloads of all the mantra and musical digital recordings to support you during meditation.

To access these files, please visit **MadhurNain.com/beyondthepain** and enter the code, BeyondThePainCollection. You will need to provide your email address. Because these files are very large, these downloads need to be completed on a computer; they will not work on a cellphone or tablet. If you have any questions, do not hesitate to reach out: info@ madhurnain.com.

GLOSSARY

Adrenal glands. A pair of glands located at the top of each kidney, responsible for controlling the secretion of hormones. Epinephrine (adrenaline) and norepinephrine (noradrenaline)—which contribute to the fight-or-flight response—are produced by the adrenal glands.

Adrenaline. See epinephrine.

Amino acids. Considered the building blocks of protein, these compounds aid in a variety of life functions, such as hormone production, neurotransmitter support, nutrient absorption, repairing body tissue, boosting the immune system, and generally offering energy source.

Amygdala. A mass of gray matter inside each cerebral hemisphere in the brain which helps us to experience emotions.

Anxiety. A nervous disorder associated with excessive uneasiness and apprehension. Compulsive behavior, and even panic attacks, are often experienced by those suffering from anxiety.

Asana. A body position or posture (often seated) used when performing yogic activity.

Aura. The electromagnetic field of energy that surrounds every living creature. A strong, radiant aura helps protect individuals from misfortune and strengthens the physical, mental, and spiritual bodies.

Autonomic nervous system. See nervous system.

Awareness. A fundamental property of the Soul and true Self, it is the pure nature of existence: the power to be consciously conscious without an object or need.

Body Drops. A Kundalini yoga technique that asks practitioners to sit down, lift their buttocks off their seated position, then drop it back down in order to shake out excess energy from within.

Bodywork. Therapeutic techniques that involve the human body in some form, whether it is acupuncture, breathwork, massage, or energy work (such as reiki).

Breathwork. Consciously controlled breathing exercises used for their therapeutic effect on the body and mind, specifically targeting stress and relaxation levels.

Central nervous system. See nervous system.

Chakra. An energy center of consciousness, located at various points within the body, which affects life on a physical, emotional, and behavioral level.

Depression. A mental condition in which one experiences severe feelings of despondency and dejection. Often in coordination with guilt and inadequacy, depression is a deep state of melancholia that can last well beyond the typical sensation of sadness.

Dopamine. A neurotransmitter and hormone that is released when one experiences pleasure; also known as the "rewards chemical." It is also associated with motor function, mood, and decision-making.

Emotional blunting. A numbing of emotional experiences. This may result in feelings of detachment, as one is unable to fully feel and express emotions (both positive and negative) mentally, physically, and behaviorally.

Endorphins. Hormones secreted in the brain and nervous system that serve a number of physiological functions. Endorphins influence the opiate receptors, which bring us to a euphoric state and can also act as a natural painkiller.

Epinephrine. A hormone secreted by the adrenal glands that prepares us for a fight-or-flight response. It increases blood circulation and breathing in anticipation of exertion during conflicts. Also known as adrenaline.

Eye movement desensitization and reprocessing (EMDR). A form of psychotherapy that asks patients to move their eyes a specific way while processing traumatic memories. The bilateral stimulation utilized in this mental health technique helps reduce the vividness of emotions in relation to past events, ultimately alleviating the distress associated with them.

Fight-or-flight response. An instinctive physiological response to threatening situations; our bodies naturally decide to face the threat or to run away, depending on the variables. Some may find they try to "freeze" or "fix" the situation.

Gray matter. The darker tissue of the brain and spinal cord, consisting mainly of nerve cell bodies and branching dendrites. This area of the brain is where synapses occur and allows us to process information.

Helper syndrome. When one is emotionally affected by the drama and/or trauma of another individual, especially to the detriment of their own mental health.

Hydrotherapy. A form of physical therapy that incorporates water into the healing process, stimulating blood flow (usually through cold water) and supporting the nervous system.

Internal Family Systems (IFS). A form of psychotherapy that focuses on the concept of the mind being made up of multiple sub-personalities (or families). The goal of IFS is to understand the various viewpoints of each part of the mind in order to heal the mental Self.

Intrusive thoughts. Unwanted thoughts and images that cause distress. Although often harmless, they are difficult to control and can sometimes override rational thoughts, which can then lead to anxiety.

Karma. The cosmic determination of fate, based on a person's actions in current and previous states of existence.

Kundalini yoga. A form of meditation intended to release kundalini energy. Kundalini comes from the word *kundalin*, or "coiled energy"; it is the creative potential of an individual.

Mantra. A repetition of sound and rhythm that helps the mind to focus. Man means "mind," while tra is "a wave" or the movement of the mind.

Meditation. The act of thinking deeply or focusing on one's mind for a period of time, in silence or with the aid of chanting, for religious or spiritual purposes or as a method of relaxation.

Mudra. A hand position used when performing yogic activity, used to guide the body's energy flow in a particular pattern.

Negative (Protective) Mind. See Three Minds.

Nervous system. The network of nerve cells and fibers that transmits nerve impulses between parts of the body: the autonomic nervous system is the part of the nervous system responsible for the control of body functions not consciously directed, such as breathing, the heartbeat, and digestive processes; the central nervous system is the complex of nerve tissues that control the activities of the body; the peripheral nervous system is the system outside the brain and spine.

Neurotransmitters. A chemical substance released at the end of a nerve fiber by the firing off a nerve impulse, causing the transfer of cerebral information.

Neutral (Meditative) Mind. See Three Minds.

Noradrenaline. See norepinephrine.

Norepinephrine. A hormone released by the adrenal glands and sympathetic nerves, usually activated during the fight-or-flight response. Also known as noradrenaline.

Panic attack. A sudden and often debilitating fear response stemming from acute anxiety. It manifests itself in physical reactions such as heart palpitations, shaking, sweating, and shortness of breath.

Parasympathetic nervous system. A term relating to the autonomic nervous system that counterbalances the actions of the sympathetic nerves. It is responsible for the rest-and-digest part of our internal functions, neutralizing stress levels and allowing for a decreased heart rate.

Peripheral nervous system. See nervous system.

Positive (Projective) Mind. See Three Minds.

Psychotherapy. The treatment of various medical conditions by utilizing talk therapy, allowing therapists to identify troubling thoughts, feelings, and/or behaviors and offer appropriate resources to alter unwanted mental conditions.

Secondary consciousness. The ability to be self-aware, also known as higher consciousness. Expanding upon primary consciousness (perception and emotion), secondary consciousness requires an individual to apply abstract thoughts like accessing personal history and willpower.

Self. The idea that we are each our own unique individual. We are secure in the Self: present, accountable, and not checked out from our own identity.

Serotonin. A neurotransmitter and hormone that, upon release, leaves one with a "feel good" sensation due to its influence on mood and behavior.

Somatic. Relating specifically to the body, distinct from the mind.

Somatic experiencing (SE). A form of therapy that utilizes mind-body techniques in order to release damaging emotions related to past traumatic experiences. Clients are often encouraged to practice physical therapy, including breathwork and dance, to treat stress-related disorders.

Soul Self. The spirit energy that exists within us from birth. It is an inner light which we can cultivate to shine brightly, thus displaying our core and innate gifts. Also known as Soul.

Soul. See Soul Self.

Survivor's guilt. A mental and emotional condition in which one feels guilt or remorse over an incident where others experienced loss in some form. This could be in response to a life-ending accident or even the loss of material goods.

Sympathetic nervous system. The part of the autonomic nervous system that consists of nerves arising from the ganglia that helps to balance the parasympathetic nervous system. Because of its influence on the internal organs, blood vessels, and gland, the sympathetic part of our nervous system controls our energy levels (through increased heart rate and blood pressure).

Three Minds. The three mental bodies in which one can view and approach life: the Negative (Protective) Mind serves to protect us as it calculates the risks in our lives (when it is weak, we make poor decisions); the Positive (Projective) Mind is where we weigh the risk versus reward ratio (when it is weak, our impulsive energy takes over in order to see quick results); and the Neutral (Meditative) Mind, which is the harmonious balance between the Negative and Positive Minds.

Toxic shame. A feeling of worthlessness and self-loafing, toxic shame manifests itself into internal dialogues like, "I am a bad person because I did a bad thing" instead of, "I am a good person who did a bad thing."

Unconscious trauma. Distressing memories caused by traumatic experiences that are stored in the subconscious mind. Reactions and responses to certain events are often detrimentally reflected by these hidden or inaccessible memories.

Vagus nerve. A vital component of the parasympathetic nervous system, vagal nerves carry signals between the brain, heart, and digestive system. Its function is to calm the body after experiencing stress.

Vitality. The energy force within us that acts as the fuel for life because it gives us purpose. When we have vitality, we have a sense of completeness and contentment; it helps us to feel alive and present.

White matter. The paler tissue of the brain and spinal cord, consisting mainly of myelinated axons that carry information gathered from gray matter.

Wise Self. See Wise-Adult Self.

Wise-Adult Self. The form of the Self in which we grow into with our accumulated knowledge and experience of life. In this form, we are less reactive, more responsive, less rigid, more flexible, less closed off, more open and accepting; in essence, a wise and functioning adult. Also known as Wise Self.

Yoga. A discipline that includes breathwork, meditation, and the use of certain body and/or hand postures that are used for health or relaxation.

Young Self. See Young-Adult Self.

Young-Adult Self. The form of the Self in which we are between our child parts and our Wise-Adult Self. This is the stage of life where we are the most reactive due to self-protection. Although it is a precarious stage, it can be enjoyable to exist as the Young-Adult Self because we have a great capacity to learn. Also known as Young Self.

ACKNOWLEDGMENTS

FIRST AND FOREMOST, THANK you to my curious clients who have trusted me on their healing journey. It isn't easy to deal with grief, whether you have lost a loved one, felt betrayed in some way, or generally feel like the world is against you. It is through the vulnerability of my clients that I have been able to witness every nuanced stage of disappointment. Recognizing that it is a part of life, I know that we all can move through it in our own way—as long as we do the work.

Thank you to my husband, Julian, who has supported me through anything and everything that I have wanted to embark on throughout this experience we call life. Your love and constant presence have offered me consistent stability.

I am so very thankful for my two sons. As I always say, they are my greatest teachers because they constantly encourage me to ask big questions. Through their challenging of me, and their courage to find and build upon their path in life, they inspire me to look deep within myself and my own path. Because of my unconditional love for them, I am always willing to self-reflect and self-correct. Life takes work, and my love for my sons gives me the focus and energy to put in the effort.

Thank you to my parents. I am continuously inspired by their own journey through life and their search for meaning, including making commitments and following through with them. They have had to endure hardship and pain within their community, difficulties spanning 50 years. Yet despite that, they have been able to find their truth about life again and make necessary changes. It's been incredible to see them let go of dogmatic practices once instilled deep within them, only to come fully into their own in their mid-70s. They are proof that it's never too late to keep learning, growing, loving, and believing. I am thankful to have you as my parents.

Thank you to my personal editor, Kristina Sigler, who has been on this book-writing endeavor with me for over seven years. I honor her with her insight, hard work, and how she supports my vision. She has helped provide the creative development of the gifts I want to share with the world.

Thank you to Alex Dolven, the producer of the meditation music shared with this book. We have been creating beautiful meditation music together since 2014.

Thank you to Alexus Kearney, who photographed my headshot and created the original cover art for this book. I have loved working with you over these past ten years; your eye for design has helped me bring my projects to life. Also thank you to Guru Amrit Kaur Khalsa from Norway who illustrated the meditation and yoga poses provided on my website.

Thank you to the team at Hatherleigh Press who took a chance with me by bringing my book to the world. Thank you especially to Ryan Kennedy, who worked on the final edits; and Ryan Tumambing, who navigated the marketing and release of this book. It takes a team to create and deliver a book to publication.

Finally, thank you to everyone who has ever believed in me and supported me.

BIBLIOGRAPHY

"Anger -How It Affects People." Better Health Channel, 2012, www.betterhealth.vic.gov.au/health/healthyliving/anger-how-it-affects-people.

Brené Brown. *The Gifts of Imperfection: 10th Anniversary Edition*. Random House, 2020.

Brennan, Dan. "Mental Health Benefits of Journaling." WebMD, 25 Oct. 2021, www.webmd.com/mental-health/mental-health-benefits-of-journaling.

Caplin, Andrew, and John Leahy. Wishful Thinking (March 2019). NBER Working Paper No. w25707, ssrn.com/abstract=3363445.

Celestine, Nicole. "The Science of Happiness in Positive Psychology 101." PositivePsychology.com, 26 Jan. 2017, positivepsychology.com/happiness/.

Csikszentmihalyi, Mihaly. Flow: The Psychology of Optimal Experience. Harper Perennial Modern Classics, 1 July 2008.

Doughty, Chase. "The Feeling of Loneliness and Its Impact on Physical Health." SelectHealth.org, selecthealth.org/blog/2020/12/loneliness-and-its-impact-on-physical-health.

Frankl, Viktor. *Man's Search for Meaning*. Pocket, 1946. Gilbert, Elizabeth. Big Magic. Penguin, 22 Sept. 2015.

Gillette, Hope. "Are You Emotionally Numb? Symptoms and Possible Meanings." Psych Central, 25 Aug. 2022, psychcentral.com/ health/ signs-someone-is-emotionally-numb.

Hogan, Lilianna. "How Denial Affects Your Life." WebMD, 14 Sept. 2021, www.webmd.com/mental-health/features/ how-denial-affects-your-life.

Hyman, Mark. *The UltraMind Solution: The Simple Way to Defeat Depression, Overcome Anxiety, and Sharpen Your Mind.* New York, NY, Scribner, 8 May 2010.

"Hypertension and Your Mental Health." Westmed Family Healthcare, www.westmedfamilyhealthcare.com/blog/ hypertension-and-your-mental-health.

Katie, Byron, and Stephen Mitchell. *Loving What Is: Four Questions That Can Change Your Life.* Three Rivers Press, 23 Dec. 2023.

Klussman, Kristine. "Connecting with Your Physical Self." Wise Brain Bulletin, Wellspring Institute for Neuroscience and Contemplative Wisdom, 2021, www.wisebrain.org/bulletin/volume-15-3/ connecting-with-your-physical-self. Excerpt from Connection: How to Find the Life You're Looking for in the Life You Have by Kristine Klussman.

Lavrusheva, Olga. "The Concept of Vitality. Review of the Vitality-Related Research Domain." New Ideas in Psychology, vol. 56, no. 100752, Jan. 2020. ISSN 0732-118X, https://doi.org/10.1016/j. newideapsych.2019.100752.

Levine, Peter A., & Frederick Ann. *Waking the Tiger: Healing Trauma.* North Atlantic Books, 7 July 1997.

Lindberg, Sara. "What Is Emotional Numbing?" Verywell Mind, 11 Dec. 2007, www.verywellmind.com/ emotional-numbing-symptoms-2797372.

Lukianoff, Greg, and Jonathan Haidt. *The Coddling of the American Mind: How Good Intentions and Bad Ideas Are Setting up a Generation for Failure*. United Kingdom, Penguin Books, 2019.

Luskin, Fred. *Forgive for Good: A Proven Prescription for Health and Happiness*. San Francisco, HarperOne, 2003.

Maté, Gabor. "Helper Syndrome." Psychotherapy Networker, Sept./ Oct. 2021, www.psychotherapynetworker.org/article/helper-syndrome.

Miller, Christopher W.T. "Anger Overwhelms Our Thinking Brain. Here's How to Bring It Back Online." Washington Post, 29 Sept. 2023, www.washingtonpost.com/wellness/2023/09/29/anger-management-techniques/.

Mooventhan, A, and L Nivethitha. "Scientific Evidence-Based Effects of Hydrotherapy on Various Systems of the Body." North American Journal of Medical Sciences, vol. 6, no. 5, May 2014, p. 199, www. ncbi.nlm.nih.gov/pmc/articles/PMC4049052/, https://doi.org/10.4103/1947-2714.132935.

Open Heart. Directed by Jonathan Hock, Netflix, 2023.

Oppland, Mike. "8 Traits of Flow according to Mihaly Csikszentmihalyi." PositivePsychology.com, 16 Dec. 2016, positivepsychology.com/mihaly-csikszentmihalyi-father-of-flow/.

Pietrangelo, Ann. "The Effects of Depression in Your Body." Healthline, 30 Sept. 2014, www.healthline.com/health/depression/effects-on-body.

Real, Terrence. *The New Rules of Marriage: What You Need to Know to Make Love Work*. New York, Ballantine Books, 2008.

Real, Terrence. *Us: Getting Past You and Me to Build a More Loving Relationship*. New York, Goop Press/Rodale, 2022.

Schimelpfening, Nancy. "How to Know When Your Depression Is Getting Better." Verywell Mind, 2019, www.verywellmind.com/how-do-i-know-if-my-depression-is-getting-better-1066881.

"Shock Information | Mount Sinai -New York." Mount Sinai Health System, www.mountsinai.org/health-library/condition/shock.

Skurat, Kate. "What Is Emotional Numbness? Symptoms and Possible Causes." Calmerry, 10 Jan. 2023, calmerry.com/blog/emotions/what-is-emotional-numbness/.

Strong, Debbie. "7 Ways Anger Is Ruining Your Health." Everyday Health, 29 May 2015, www.everydayhealth.com/news/ways-anger-ruining-your-health/.

Stutz, Phil, and Barry Michels. The Tools. Random House, 21 May 2013. "The Psychological Benefits of Writing." Sparring Mind, 5 May 2014, www.sparringmind.com/benefits-of-writing/.

Trivedi, Madhukar H. "The Link between Depression and Physical Symptoms." The Primary Care Companion to the Journal of Clinical Psychiatry, vol. 6, no. Suppl 1, 2004, pp. 12–16, www.ncbi.nlm.nih. gov/pmc/articles/PMC486942/.

Tronick, Ed, and Claudia M. Gold. *The Power of Discord: Why the Ups and Downs of Relationships Are the Secret to Building Intimacy, Resilience, and Trust.* Little, Brown Spark, 2 May 2020.

Webster, Madhur-Nain. *The Stressless Brain.* Balboa Press, 10 July 2018.

Webster, Madhur-Nain. *The Stressless Brain, 2nd Edition.* B Flat Production, Oct. 2023.

Whelan, Corey. "How to Manage Low Self-Esteem." Healthline, 5 Oct. 2022, www.healthline.com/health/low-self-esteem.

Wolynn, Mark. *It Didn't Start with You: How Inherited Family Trauma Shapes Who We Are and How to End the Cycle.* Penguin Publishing Group, 25 Apr. 2017.

ABOUT THE AUTHOR

MADHUR-NAIN WEBSTER IS A licensed marriage and family therapist who prides herself on adapting different modalities of healing to meet her clients' needs. Thanks to her perceptive viewpoint, a major component of her therapeutic process involves the integration of Eastern and Western perspectives by incorporating mindfulness-based stress reduction techniques like meditation with psychotherapy interventions, such as Eye Movement Desensitization & Reprocessing (EMDR), Internal Family System (IFS), and Relational Life Therapy (RLT). A certified amino acid therapist, she also supports the use of natural methods for mental health.

Applying her lifelong experience with and knowledge of yogic technology, Madhur-Nain's therapeutic approach includes empowering clients with the ability of introspection so they can better connect with themselves and with others. By developing open communication skills, she believes an individual can understand and accept polarizing thoughts no matter their source. "It is not what happens to you," she asserts.

"It is how you make sense of it." For over 20 years, she has helped people discover and build their self-trust with excellent results.

Aspiring to reach an international audience, Madhur-Nain has continuously held yoga and meditation workshops worldwide (virtually and in-person), appeared as a guest speaker on numerous podcasts, and released over 60 meditation singles. Her chants include a variety of religious prayers and psychological affirmations, making them an inclusive form of mental health healing. Her first book, *The Stressless Brain* (2018), is an accessible scientific argument for the positive influence meditation has on the psyche.

Madhur-Nain currently runs a successful private practice in Napa, California, where she lives with her husband. In addition to her marriage of over 25 years, her greatest accomplishment is being a mother to her two adult sons. Her hobbies include traveling and expressing her creativity through clothing and jewelry design.

If you are interested in working with Madhur-Nain, please visit her website (MadhurNain.com) or email her directly (info@madhurnain.com). Whether you are looking for a short talk or a three-day retreat (online or in a designated space), she is available for speaking engagements. These workshops are ideal to build better communication skills, remove creative blocks, and inspire safer workplace environments for companies or other team settings.

To stay connected with Madhur-Nain—including new book releases, workshops (virtual and/or in-person), or meditation-related content (including music and other tools)—please join her email list on her website. If you are interested in bulk ordering her book(s), inquire by contacting her directly. She looks forward to hearing from you!